D1202864

Buffy
the vampire slayer™

HARM

SLAYERS: Why they HATE America

HARM'S CLOSET:

BEYOND GOTH TO GLAM

DOES HE WANT TO SIRE YOU?

HOW TO TELL FOR SURE!

Buffy the Vampire Slayer

Vampire Celebrity Poker—A Real High Stakes Game

HARM'S GUIDE TO SUNLESS TANNING!

Look Dusky, Not Dusty

SEASON EIGHT VOLUME 5

PREDATORS AND PREY

"Harmonic Divergence"
Script JANE ESPENSON
Pencils GEORGES JEANTY

"Swell"
Script STEVEN S. DEKNIGHT
Pencils GEORGES JEANTY

"Predators and Prey"
Script DREW Z. GREENBERG
Pencils GEORGES JEANTY

"Safe"
Script JIM KRUEGER
Pencils CLIFF RICHARDS

"Living Doll"
Script DOUG PETRIE
Pencils GEORGES JEANTY

Inks ANDY OWENS
Colors MICHELLE MADSEN
Letters RICHARD STARKINGS & COMICRAFT'S JIMMY BETANCOURT

Cover Art JO CHEN

Executive Producer JOSS WHEDON

Dark Horse Books®

President & Publisher MIKE RICHARDSON

Editor SCOTT ALLIE

Associate Editor SIERRA HAHN

Assistant Editor FREDDYE LINS

Collection Designer HEIDI WHITCOMB

This story takes place after the end of the television series *Buffy the Vampire Slayer*, created by Joss Whedon.

Special thanks to Debbie Olshan at Twentieth Century Fox and Natalie Farrell.

EXECUTIVE VICE PRESIDENT Neil Hankerson • CHIEF FINANCIAL OFFICER Tom Weddle • VICE PRESIDENT OF PUBLISHING Randy Stradley • VICE PRESIDENT OF BUSINESS DEVELOPMENT Michael Martens • VICE PRESIDENT OF MARKETING, SALES, AND LICENSING Anita Nelson • VICE PRESIDENT OF PRODUCT DEVELOPMENT David Scroggy • VICE PRESIDENT OF INFORMATION TECHNOLOGY Dale LaFountain • DIRECTOR OF PURCHASING Darlene Vogel • GENERAL COUNSEL Ken Lizzi EDITORIAL DIRECTOR Davey Estrada • SENIOR MANAGING EDITOR Scott Allie • SENIOR BOOKS EDITOR, DARK HORSE BOOKS Chris Warner • EXECUTIVE EDITOR Diana Schutz • DIRECTOR OF DESIGN AND PRODUCTION Cary Grazzini ART DIRECTOR Lia Ribacchi • DIRECTOR OF SCHEDULING Cara Niece

BUFFY THE VAMPIRE SLAYER™ VOLUME FIVE: PREDATORS AND PREY

Buffy the Vampire Slayer™ & © 1998, 2009 Twentieth Century Fox Film Corporation. All rights reserved. Buffy™ and all other prominently featured characters are trademarks of Twentieth Century Fox Film Corporation. Dark Horse Books® and the Dark Horse logo are registered trademarks of Dark Horse Comics, Inc. All rights reserved. No portion of this publication may be reproduced or transmitted, in any form or by any means, without the express written permission of Dark Horse Comics, Inc. Names, characters, places, and incidents featured in this publication either are the product of the author's imagination or are used fictitiously. Any resemblance to actual persons (living or dead), events, institutions, or locales, without satiric intent, is coincidental.

This volume reprints the comic-book series *Buffy the Vampire Slayer* Season Eight #21–#25 and short stories from *MySpace Dark Horse Presents* #18 and #19 from Dark Horse Comics.

Published by
Dark Horse Books
A division of
Dark Horse Comics, Inc.
10956 SE Main Street
Milwaukie, OR 97222

darkhorse.com

To find a comics shop in your area,
call the Comic Shop Locator Service toll-free at (888) 266-4226.

First edition: September 2009
ISBN 978-1-59582-342-7

1 3 5 7 9 10 8 6 4 2

Printed in the United States of America

Ladies
@ Club

HARMONIC

DIVERGENCE

elite
SORRY, MA'AM, CAN'T HELP YOU.
OH, CAN YOU REALLY SAY NO TO THIS PERKY PAIR?
NO ANIMALS IN THE CLUB.
C'MON, GIRLS.
"OOH. SOMEONE FAMOUS! I'VE GOT URINE RUNNING DOWN MY LEG!"

WHO IS HE?
"HERE'S THE THING ABOUT FAME. IT'S GOOD TO TOUCH."
IT'S LINDSAY LOHAN'S MOTHER!

"I'M GONNA TOUCH SOME FAME!"
KLICK
FLASH

"CHECK OUT HOW
HOT I LOOK!

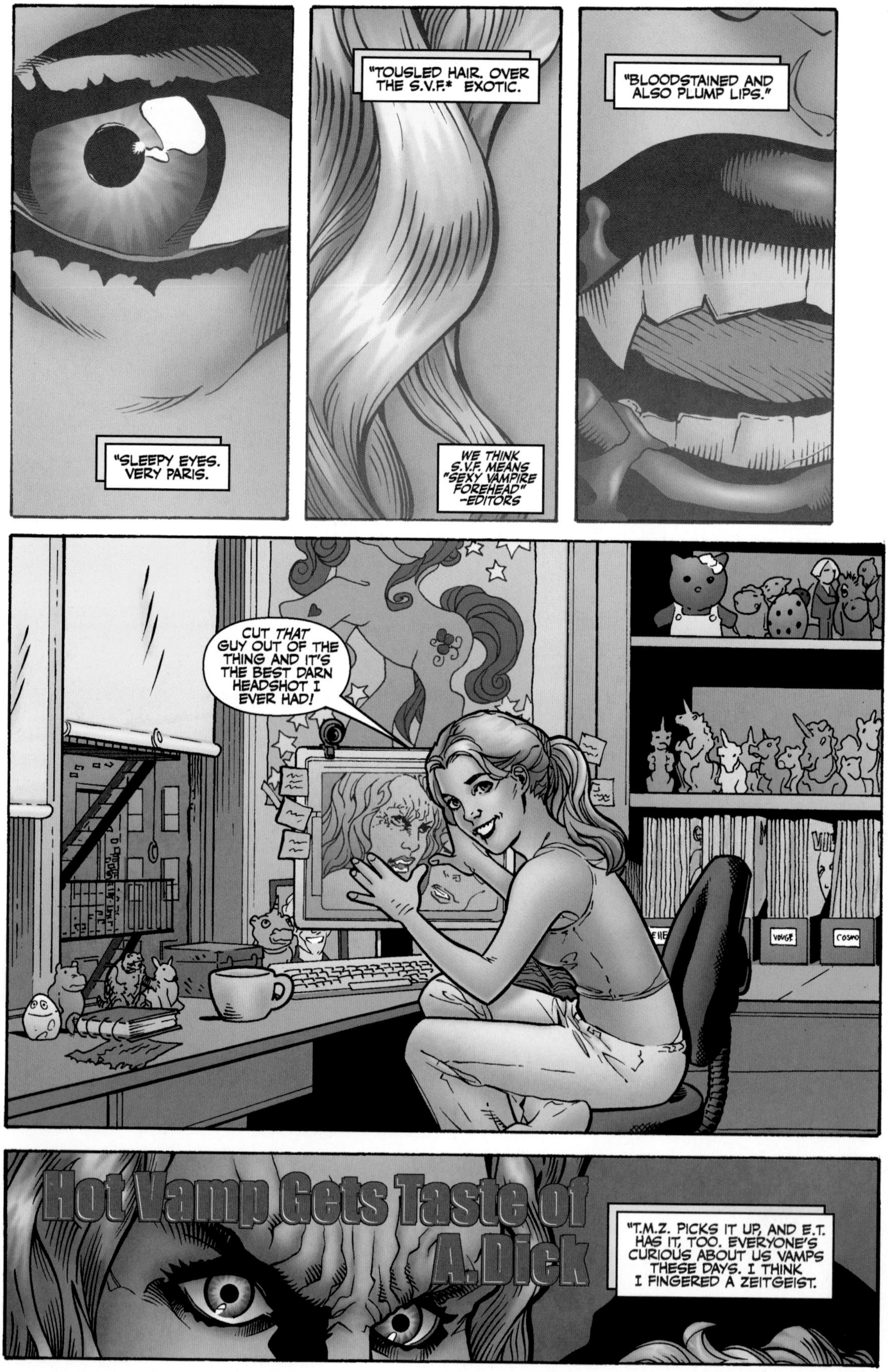

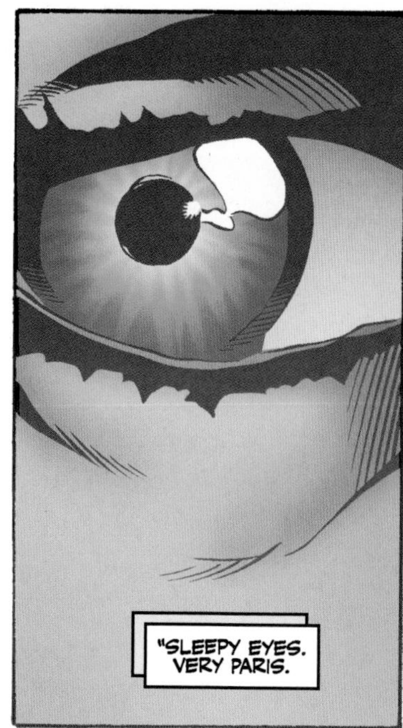

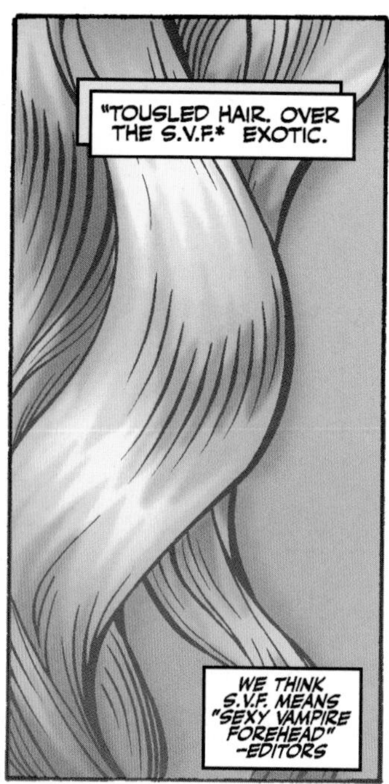

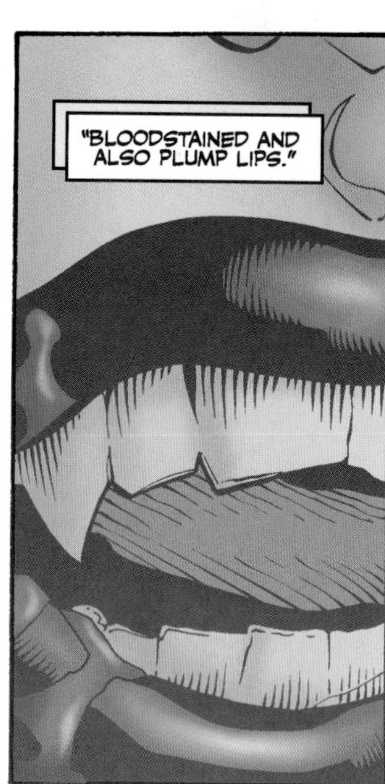

CUT *THAT* GUY OUT OF THE THING AND IT'S THE BEST DARN HEADSHOT I EVER HAD!

"THIS IS C.A.A. NO ONE KNOWS WHAT THAT STANDS FOR, BUT IT'S A BIG SCARY BUILDING WITH A HOLE IN IT AND IT'S FULL OF AGENTS. THEY WORK LATE."
2000

EXCUSE ME, AGENT?

"A LOT OF GUYS DON'T KNOW YOU CAN GET BITTEN BUT NOT DIE. WHEN THEY FIND THAT OUT, THEY'RE ALL CURIOUS.

Ding

"HE AGREED TO SET UP A COUPLE MEETINGS.

"THIS IS THE M.T.V. BUILDING IN SANTA MONICA. NO ONE KNOWS WHAT THAT STANDS FOR EITHER, BUT THEY DO REALITY SHOWS. THEY AGREED TO MEET AFTER SUNSET."
MTV NETWORKS

...AND YOU CAN JUST FOLLOW ME AROUND, AND WATCH MY LIFE, SEE ME WITH MY FRIENDS WHO YOU CAN CAST PEOPLE FOR AND I'LL MOSTLY BE BITING PEOPLE AT WILD PARTIES AND YOU CAN CALL IT HARMONY BITES!
"PITCHING IS FUN!"

HMM... I DUNNO. SEEMS LIKE IT NEEDS A VILLAIN.
NO, SEE, THAT'S THE HOOK!

WITH ME, YOU GET A HERO...

WITH A VILLAIN BUILT IN!
"I HAVE A TELEVISION SHOW!

"I HAVE A CAMERA CREW!

"I HAVE A STORY LINE!

"THE NUMBERS ARE SOFT, BUT I THINK WE CAN TURN IT AROUND. WE'RE GOING TO PUT MORE MONEY INTO PROMOTIONS. I'M GOING TO BE IN *PEOPLE!*"
MTV VAMPING FOR TIME; BAD TIMING FOR
WHAT THE HELL?
PFFFT. SHE'S NO TINA FEY.
"SEXIEST GIRL (NOT) ALIVE"

"THEY EVEN GIVE ME BILLBOARDS. OLD MEDIA SUCKS BUT SO DO I, L.O.L."
Harmony Bites
MTV 7pm Weeknights

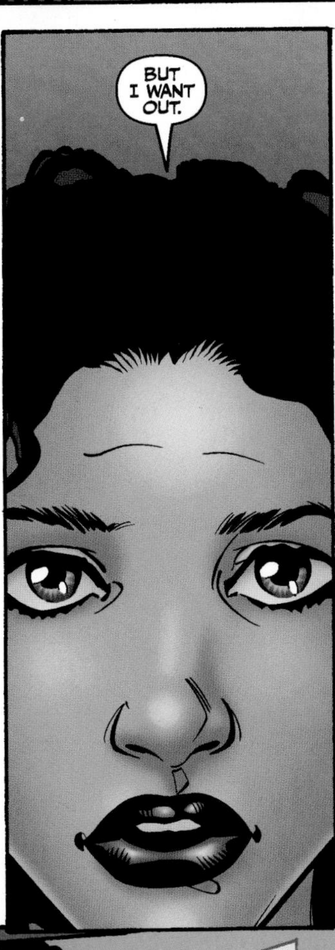
BUT I WANT OUT.

I FINALLY SAY IT ON MY SIXTEENTH BIRTHDAY.

THE OTHER GIRLS AREN'T TAKING IT TOO GOOD.
THOK

OOONF!
BONG
WELL. THIS CHANGES STUFF.

I FEEL TOTALLY FREE.

BUT I FIGURE IT WON'T LAST.

IF I KNOW ANYTHING ABOUT GOOD LUCK, IT'S THAT SOMEONE ALWAYS SHOWS UP TO TAKE IT AWAY.
LCD FLAT SCREEN
I CAN'T CONTROL MY STRENGTH! AND I'M HAVING DREAMS THAT ARE STRANGE AND DISTURB ME.
New
$ LCD

DREAMS OF BEING ANOTHER GIRL, IN ANOTHER TIME?
I'M NOT GONNA GO FIND THEM. IF THEY WANT ME, THEY HAVE TO FIND ME.

A WEEK LATER...

HI. CAN WE TALK ABOUT YOUR DESTINY?
OH, CRAP.

LET US TALK OF THE VAMPYRS.

I HEARD THEY CAN BITE YOU WITHOUT KILLING YOU. SO WHAT'S THE HARM?
OH, SEÑORITA, YOU HAVE A LOT TO LEARN.

THEY ARE WITHOUT CONSCIENCE! NO SENSE OF EMPATHY, NO CONNECTION TO THE SORROWS OF OTHERS! UNDEAD SOULLESS CREATURES OF THE DARK!
UH-HUH.
THEY TAKE ADVANTAGE OF THE WEAK ONES...

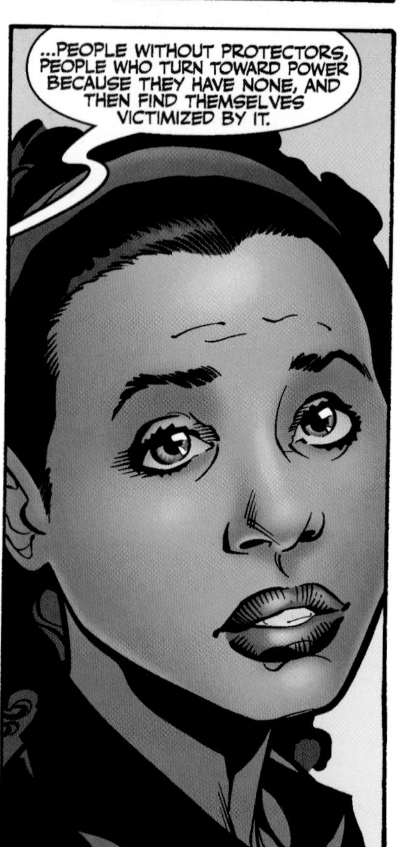
...PEOPLE WITHOUT PROTECTORS, PEOPLE WHO TURN TOWARD POWER BECAUSE THEY HAVE NONE, AND THEN FIND THEMSELVES VICTIMIZED BY IT.

I'M IN. WHERE ARE THEY AND HOW BAD CAN I KILL 'EM?
I'LL CALL BUFFY. SHE'LL WANT TO WELCOME YOU.

HELLO?

THE GIRL TALKS A LOT, BUT IT'S KIND OF A CRAPPY CONNECTION.
HONOR... BRFFFF... DUTY. TOGETHER... OVER BZZT DEATH... EVIL CANDY... SOMETIMES THERE ARE SNAKES... HONOR.

WE'LL PROTECT YOU. WE'LL TRAIN YOU. YOU'LL BE PART OF A FAMILY...

TOGETHERNESS! UNITY! SISTERHOOD!

I UNDERSTAND THOSE WORDS. I'VE HEARD 'EM BEFORE.
HARMONY BITES
MTV 7PM WEEKNIGHTS

I THINK SHE HUNG UP.
I'LL SLAY THE HELL OUT OF VAMPIRES. BUT I AIN'T JOINING NO OTHER BUNCH OF GIRLS. I'M DOING THIS ALONE.

I DON'T EVEN LIKE THE MEMBERSHIP CARD I STILL GOT.
Las Cuchillas

Do You Ink I'm Sexy
DO YOU INK I'M SEXY
TATTOO
CAN I SEE?

BETTER.

OOH! CLEM! LOOK AT THIS PLACE! IT'S SO AUTHENTIC AND GRUBBY!

VERY DOWNWARD-SPIRAL CHIC.

WHAT THE PINK HELL IS *THIS?*
IT'S HARMONY. YOU KNOW HER SHOW, ***HARMONY BITES,*** RIGHT?
UM... NO.
THAT'S OKAY. IT'S PROBABLY NOT GONNA MAKE IT. REALITY SHOW ABOUT A VAMPIRE, ONLY NOTHING MUCH EVER HAPPENS.

ARE YOU GETTING A TATTOO? YOU SHOULD GET A TATTOO.
A VAMPIRE?

I DUNNO...
EVERYONE LIKES A FLAMING FLYING SKULL.

I HAVE A LITTLE CARTOON DUCK... SOMEWHERE...
SO, UM, WHAT IF I WANTED TO TALK TO HARMONY ALONE?

I DUNNO ABOUT ALONE, BUT WE SHOOT AT A RENTED HOUSE, UP IN THE HILLS. YOU CAN COME ON BY IF YOU WANT. WE NEED HOT EXTRAS FOR A PARTY SCENE TONIGHT.

I LIKE A PARTY.

SEEMS FUNNY TO ME. SECURITY WORKING A PARTY WHERE EVERYONE'S HOPING TO GET BIT BY A MONSTER.

BUT STILL, THEY'RE NOT HAPPY WITH A FOOTLONG PIECE OF SPLINTERED LUMBER.

NICE... THAT A BITE?
WHAT? OH, NO. IT'S NOT A BITE.

OH. MAYBE YOU'LL GET LUCKY TONIGHT, THOUGH. IT'S FUN WHEN IT HAPPENS. IT'S LIKE, YOU FEEL WEAKER, BUT YOU FEEL LIKE THAT'S OKAY.

WE'RE GONNA BRING IN HARMONY AND SOME OF THE MAJOR PLAYERS IN A LITTLE BIT, BUT FIRST WE'RE GONNA SHOOT YOU GUYS JUST HAVING A GOOD TIME, OKAY?
NOW, THE MUSIC'S GONNA BE LOUD UNTIL HARMONY COMES IN, THEN IT'LL BE REAL SOFT SO WE CAN HEAR WHATEVER SHE MIGHT DO...

...NOW *PARTY! WHOO!*

GIRL'S AROUND HERE SOMEWHERE. AND I NEED A STAKE...
IT'S MY PARTY AND I CAN HAVE MORE THAN ONE DATE IF I WANT TO!
I DON'T KNOW IF YOU DESERVE THAT.
BUT I WANT TO BE SOMETHING SPECIAL TO YOU! COME ON, TURN ME INTO A VAMPIRE LIKE YOU AND WE CAN BE TOGETHER FOREVER!
DON'T LOOK AT HER. DON'T LOOK INTO THE CAMERA. COME ON, KEEP DANCING!
A STAKE... A STAKE... SOMETHING HAS TO BE WOOD.
HEY!
RMONY BITES
18

Skplinta
YIIIP?
GLOMM
OW!
THOMP
OOMFF.

KRAK

DIRTY STINKING BLOODSUCKER. THESE ARE KIDS!

CHONK!

KRAK
"OH, MY ACHIN' ANKLES.
"I'M TERRIFIED. THIS GIRL IS CLEARLY A SLAYER.
THNK
"PEOPLE ARE GONNA LIKE SLAYERS, RIGHT? THIS COULD REALLY HURT MY SHOW."
SHHK

SNNNRRRRL...

SNNNRRRRL...

SNNNRRRRL...
THAT'S NOT ENTERTAINMENT!

OH MY GOD.
SNNNRRRRL...
VARIETY.COM SAYS IT'S MAKING RATINGS HISTORY AND SETTING DOWNLOAD RECORDS.

AND IT MADE M.T.V. THE HIGHEST-RATED CABLE NETWORK LAST NIGHT, AND SECOND OVERALL, TRAILING ONLY AMERICAN IDOL. IT'S A PHENOMENON!
ALL THE SHOW NEEDED WAS A VILLAIN!

AND NOW WE HAVE THOUSANDS OF THEM. WE'RE DOING SOME INVESTIGATING, BUT IT SEEMS LIKE THERE'S A WHOLE SLAYER ARMY. VERY ORGANIZED, VERY VIOLENT. BEST VILLAINS SINCE THE NAZIS! BETTER!
YAY!
SCHEDULE
"WHO WANTS TO BE SIRED?"
"FLAVOR OF BLOOD"
"UNDEAD CHEF"
"PROJECT VAMPIRE"

"BETTER THAN NAZIS! CAN YOU FEEL THE ZEITGEIST? IT'S ALL TINGLY!"

WHAT THE HELL IS WRONG WITH PEOPLE?

PEOPLE SUCK. OOH. ANDERSON COOPER.
SPICE WORLD

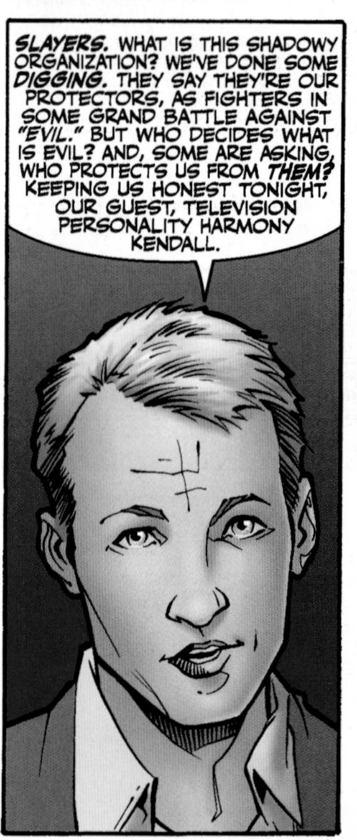
SLAYERS. WHAT IS THIS SHADOWY ORGANIZATION? WE'VE DONE SOME DIGGING. THEY SAY THEY'RE OUR PROTECTORS, AS FIGHTERS IN SOME GRAND BATTLE AGAINST "EVIL." BUT WHO DECIDES WHAT IS EVIL? AND, SOME ARE ASKING, WHO PROTECTS US FROM THEM? KEEPING US HONEST TONIGHT, OUR GUEST, TELEVISION PERSONALITY HARMONY KENDALL.

COOPER
360
YOU PROMISED TO INTRODUCE...
AND HER DOG, QUEEN PUFFLES OF POMERANIA.

DID YOU HEAR ANDERSON COOPER ON THE T.V.?
BUFFY, IT SEEMS LIKE THE WORLD DOESN'T KNOW WE'RE THE GOOD GUYS.
NO. THEY DO. THEY HAVE TO. RIGHT? THEY CAN TELL WHO'S WEARING THE WHITE HATS.

The End

Swell

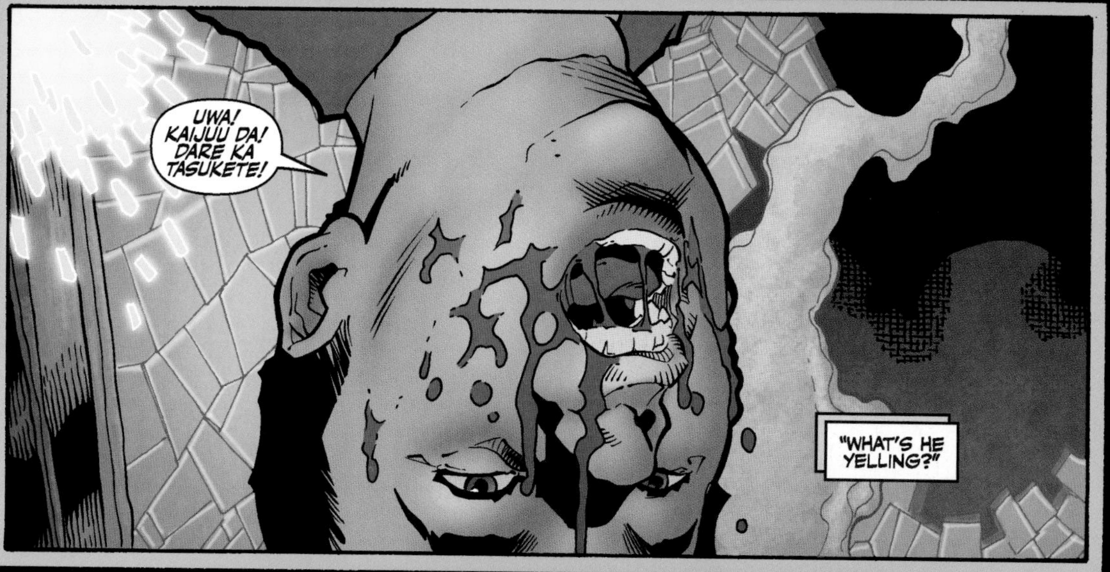

"MONSTER. BIG #%&@ING MONSTER."
UH... HOW BIG?
SATSU! TARGET ACQUIRED! BEARING NORTH-NORTHEAST!
STEER HIM AWAY FROM THE CROWDS! FORCE HIM TOWARDS THE BRIDGE!
COPY -- UFFF!
CHECK ON AYUMI. TELL HER TRY DUCKING NEXT TIME.
WHAT'S YOUR PLAN?
BLOOD.
SCREAMING.
THE USUAL.

OH CRAP...
SANTORIO CORP.
OH CRAP OH CRAP OH --
SLICE
CRAP!
SSSLUPK
UFFF!
ZZR

KENNEDY?!

YOU SEE THE *TAIL* ON THAT THING? *MOMMA!* YOU SHOULD TRY *DUCKING* NEXT TIME.

WHAT ARE YOU DOING HERE?

JUST IN THE NEIGHBORHOOD. I THOUGHT I'D DROP IN AND ELECTROCUTE A WHATEVER-THE-HELL-THAT-WAS.

BUFFY SENT YOU, DIDN'T SHE?

KLUDD
GRRR?
BUFFY SENDS THE *OTHER LESBIAN SLAYER* TO CHECK UP ON ME, AND I'M THE ONE YOU'RE YELLING AT?
LOOK, BUFFY DIDN'T SEND ME, OKAY? I VOLUNTEERED.
BECAUSE YOU'RE THE OTHER LESBIAN.
BECAUSE I WANTED YOU TO KNOW YOU'RE NOT THE ONLY FOOL TO EVER WRINKLE THE SHEETS WITH A STRAIGHT GIRL.
IT WASN'T JUST WRINKLES.
IT WAS TRUE LOVE.
YEAH, YEAH, EVERYBODY KNOWS THE STORY. YOUR KISS BROUGHT BUFFY OUT OF A MYSTICAL COMA.
BUT SLEEPING BEAUTY WASN'T GAY. AND NEITHER IS BUFFY.
DESPITE RECENTLY TAKING A SKINNY DIP IN THAT POOL.

IT WAS MORE THAN A DIP. IT WAS A PLUNGE. A BIG, WET--

YOU HAD A THING, I GET IT! TIME TO TOWEL OFF AND FACE THE HETERO.
YOU, GAY. BUFFY, NOT.
MY ADVICE? LOSE THE CINNAMON LIPPY GLOSS YOU LAID ON HER AND TRY KISSING SOMEONE WHO CAN GIVE YOU THEIR HEART. NOT JUST THEIR BODY.

BUT I REALLY LOVE CINNAMON.
YEAH, IT'S GREAT. BUT THERE ARE A LOT OF OTHER FLAVORS OUT THERE. MAYBE IT'S TIME TO TRY A NEW ONE.

AND THAT CONCLUDES THE MOLLYCODDLE. I WAS SENT HERE FOR AN EVAL, SO LET'S START THE UATION WITH THE OBVIOUS.
WHAT'S IN THE SACK?

"IT'S A WHAT?!"
A VAMPY CAT!
A WHO WHAT NOW?
VAMPY CAT, THE NEW HAPPY CAT VARIANT. PRE-ORDERS ARE THROUGH THE ROOF, BUT IT'S NOT SUPPOSED TO HIT THE MARKET UNTIL NEXT WEEK.
VAMPY CAT!
GRRR! ARGH!
HE'LL LOVE
THE SANTORIO
CORPORATION!
THIS ONE MUST BE A PROTOTYPE OR SOMETHING. WHICH EXPLAINS THE ARMORED CAR.
VAMPIRES AREN'T *CUTE* AND *FLUFFY!* AND A *KITTY CAT?* *COME ON!*
SINCE THAT IDIOT HARMONY'S REALITY SHOW TOOK OFF, EVERYBODY'S OBSESSED WITH FANGS AND LUMPY FOREHEADS.
PUBLIC'S SWALLOWING THEIR UNDEAD BULL BY THE HANDFUL.

"BUT WHY WOULD A FOUR-ARMED WHATCHAMACALLIT WANT TO STEAL A VAMPY CAT?"
THE SLAYER BITCH TOOK THE BAIT -- AND MY HAND!
MY BEAUTIFUL FOURTH HAND!
YOU HAVE DONE WELL, GUNYARR-SAN. AND YOU SHALL BE REWARDED...

...WITH A QUICK DEATH.

CRAP.

DUCKING IS JUST AS IMPORTANT AS THE HITTING, AYUMI. MORE. DUCK, DON'T GET HIT.
THAT THING HAD FOUR ARMS! I DUCKED THE FIRST THREE!

≶YAWN≶
PLEASE TELL ME YOUR COFFEE SUCKS LESS THAN YOUR BEDS, WHICH, B.T.W., SUCK -- OH MY GOD!
WHAT THE HELL ARE YOU WEARING?!
IT'S A FURISODE! GIRLS WEAR THEM WHEN THEY COME OF AGE TO SHOW THEY'RE SINGLE AND AVAILABLE FOR MARRIAGE.
MY PARENTS BOUGHT IT FOR ME. BEFORE I DESTROYED THEM WITH MY GAYNESS.
AH, THEY WERE SO RIGHT! THE WHOLE KISSING GIRLS THING? BLECHH!
GIRLS SHOULD KISS BOYS AND HAVE THEIR BABIES!
MMM, BABIES! WE SHOULD MAKE SOME LIKE NORMAL GIRLS, INSTEAD OF RUNNING AROUND HITTING PEOPLE ALL THE TIME. I MEAN, WHY ARE SLAYERS SO AGGRO?
WITH THE HACKING AND THE CHOPPING AND THE STAKING! WE SHOULD BE ASHAMED OF OURSELVES, BRINGING SO MUCH MISERY INTO THE WORLD!
I DON'T KNOW WHAT THE GEISHA'S GOTTEN INTO YOU, BUT MAYBE WE OUGHTA MOSEY DOWN TO YOUR RESIDENT WITCH AND --

TAKE YOUR STINKING PAWS OFF ME, YOU DAMN DIRTY SLAYER!

HEY! LET'S JUST, UH... HEY!

WE'RE NOTHING BUT A BUNCH OF SELF-RIGHTEOUS LITTLE OVARIES! WE MARCH AROUND PLAYING SOLDIER, DECIDING WHO'S EVIL AND WHO'S NOT.

WE'RE THE EVIL ONES! AND WE'RE GOING TO GET WHAT WE DESER--

KLUDD

WHUKK

HUUARRKK
I AM DISCOVERED, MY BROTHERS!
USE WHAT I HAVE GIVEN! STRIKE AT THE HEART OF THE BEAST!
AHHHH! GET IT OFF ME! GET IT --
SLIICE

WHAT JUST HAPPENED?
AND WHAT THE HELL AM I WEARING?

OH GOD, MY STOMACH...

SORRY!
MAYBE YOU SHOULD HAVE STAYED BEHIND.

SCREW THAT.
WHOLE BOTTLE OF MOUTHWASH, AND I CAN STILL TASTE THAT FURRY LITTLE BASTARD.
I WANT TO HIT SOMETHING.

A LOT.

THE ENTIRE VAMPY CAT INVENTORY SHIPPED AN HOUR AGO. THEY'RE GOING GLOBAL.

DOWNLOAD A TARGET MANIFEST. I'LL NOTIFY ALL SLAYER CELLS WITHIN RANGE --

OH GOD. HALF A MILLION OF THEM ARE ON A SHIP HEADED FOR SCOTLAND.

SCOTLAND. THAT'S WHY THE LITTLE BASTARD CLIMBED DOWN YOUR THROAT. TO GET THE LOCATION OF OUR HOME BASE.

BUFFY. THEY'RE GOING AFTER BUFFY.

SANTORIO
DAIKAIJU
SURE THAT'S ENOUGH?
IF NOT, WE'LL TRY PLAN B.
WHAT'S PLAN B?
SAME AS "A."
YOU DIE.

SLAYERS!
ATTACK, MY BROTHERS!
EAT THEIR #%&@ING OVARIES!

GAKK!
GET IN HER MOUTH! GET IN HER --
GET IN HER -- ARGHHH!
MY DEATH IS MEANINGLESS, SLAYER SCUM!
NOTHING CAN STOP THE SWELL!

THE WHAT NOW?
GARRRGHHHH!!
WE ARE THE SWELL!
WE ARE LEGION!

CLEANSED IN A SEA OF BLOOD!
TWILIGHT COMMANDS IT! HAIL, TWILIGHT!
TWILIGHT?
FIGURES A BUNCH OF STUFFED @$$HOLES WOULD BE WORKING FOR THAT TOOL.
ARHHHHH
WE WILL CRUSH YOU INTO AN ANNOYING JELLY FOR SUCH INSOLENCE!
foosh
HAHAHAHA HAHAHA!
YOU THINK YOUR LITTLE SPARKLER CAN ABATE THE FURY OF THE SWELL?!

UMM... GIANT STUFFED ANIMAL MONSTER'S GOT A POINT.

IT'S NOT THE SPARKS HE SHOULD BE AFRAID OF...

IT'S THE FIRE.

FIRE!

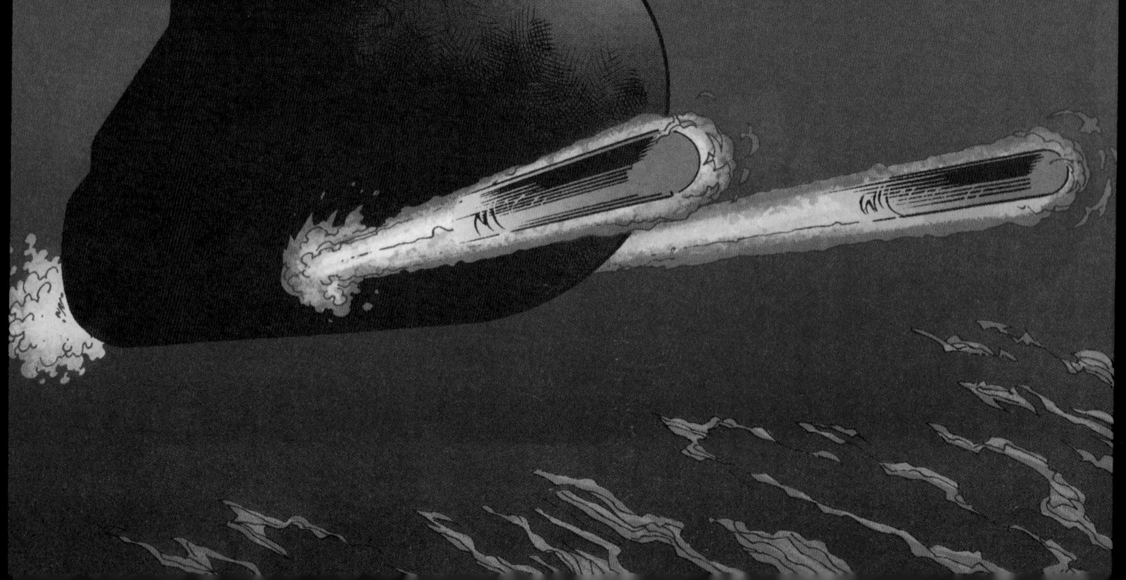

BAHOOM
AHHHARGHHH...
WHAT THE HELL WAS THAT?!
PLAN B.
YOU HAVE A FREAKIN' *SUB?!*
BUNCH OF VAMPS TOOK IT FROM THE KOREANS. I TOOK IT BACK.
YOU COULD HAVE MENTIONED THAT IN YOUR REPORT.
WAS GONNA. AFTER I GOT DONE PLAYING WITH IT.
YOUR EVAL'S *SO* GETTING A SMILEY FACE.

...ALL THE VAMPY CAT SHIPMENTS HAVE BEEN DESTROYED, ALONG WITH THE FACTORY THEY SPAWNED FROM. BUT--
THERE'S A BUT?
BIG BUTS COME WITH THE SLAYER TERRITORY THESE DAYS AND I PROBABLY SHOULD HAVE REVIEWED THAT SENTENCE BEFORE UNLEASHING IT ON THE SENSITIVE WOMENFOLK.
HEY, DON'T WE HAVE SOME TIVO FOR THESE KIDS?
THESE "SLAYERS" HACKED, BURNED, AND BLEW UP MILLIONS OF FLUFFY STUFFED KITTIES! AND WHY?
BECAUSE THEY HAD TINY LITTLE FANGS! THEY HATE US SO MUCH THEY'RE KILLING TOYS NOW!
WELL THAT'S JUST MEAN.
HARMONY KENDALL
REALITY HOST
AND VAMPIRE-RIGHTS
SPOKESWOMAN
FLUFFY STUFFED KITTIES THAT CLIMB DOWN YOUR THROAT!
AND WHY HASN'T SOMEONE INTRODUCED BLONDIE TO A POINT-HEAD STICK?
BECAUSE THE LAST THING WE NEED RIGHT NOW IS TO MAKE HARMONY A MARTYR.
EVERYONE THINKS WE'RE THE BAD GUYS. WE'LL PROVE 'EM WRONG.
BUT UNTIL THEN, WE KEEP A LOW PROFILE. LIKE SUBTERRANEAN.

HAS IT REALLY GOTTEN THAT BAD?
WE'RE HATED AND FEARED MORE THAN THE BLOODSUCKING UNDEAD. AND TWILIGHT JUST TRIED TO MURDER US ALL WITH AN ARMY OF STUFFED ANIMALS.
IT'S WAY THAT BAD.

WE NEED TO STOP BEING WHATEVER WE'VE BEEN AND FOCUS. BE MORE THAN HUMAN. OR THE LESS-THAN IS GONNA WIN.
KEEP THE SUB HANDY. I THINK WE'RE GOING TO NEED IT.

NOT THE HEY-GUESS-WHAT?-YOU-TURNED-ME-GAY SPEECH YOU WERE PROBABLY HOPING FOR, HUH?

BUFFY'S RIGHT. THE WORLD'S COMING APART. IT'S TIME TO STOP BEING WHO WE WERE...
SHOPPING?
LET'S GO SHOPPING.

...AND GET A NEW FLAVOR.
Lip Gloss
Cinnamon

The End

PREDATORS AND PREY

THE BONDS BETWEEN US ARE TIGHT AND UNBREAKABLE.
BUFFY! WHERE'S BUFFY?!
SHE'S IN THE COMMAND CENTER WITH MR. HARRIS AND MS. ROSENBERG. WHAT'S GOIN--
NO TIME!!
THANK YOU!!
I LIKE YOUR TOP!!
YOU HURT ONE OF US, YOU'RE TAKING ON ALL OF US.
IT'S LIKE OUR GUIDING PRINCIPLE. NOTHING COMES BETWEEN US.
WHAMMM!
ANDREW, IF YOU SLAM THAT DOOR ONE MORE TIME, I WILL MAKE YOU EAT IT.
CONTROL ROOM
BUFFY!

SORRY. THAT MAY HAVE COME OUT SOUNDING HARSH.
FORGIVE HER. WE'RE UP TO OUR EYEBALLS, OR, FOR SOME, EYEBALL, IN HARMONY FALLOUT.
IT'S OKAY. BUT PREPARE, MON FRÈRE AND FRÈRE-ETTES, TO HAVE YOUR DAY GET A LOT BETTER. I JUST GOT US A LEAD ON ONE SIMONE DOFFLER. WHAT UUUUUUUUUP!

SIMONE? SERIOUSLY? EVER SINCE SHE WENT ROGUE, SHE'S BEEN OFF THE GRID. HOW DID YOU FIND HER?
NOT HER. HER LIEUTENANT, NISHA. I USUALLY MONITOR DEMON ACTIVITY IN OUR HOT SPOTS, AND THIS MORNING I GOT A PING OUTSIDE MILAN.
SEEMS OUR LITTLE NISHA'S BEEN MESSING WHERE SHE SHOULDN'T HAVE BEEN MESSING, GOT SNARED IN THE TRAP OF A RAGNA SPIDER DEMON.

I'VE BEEN WANTING TO FIND SIMONE. ALL THESE REPORTS OF SHADOWY ATTACKS ON BANKS, MILITARY BASES, THE OCCASIONAL HOT TOPIC...
LAST FEW DAYS, REPORTS STARTED COMING IN MORE FREQUENTLY. BANDIT GANG OF WOMEN, ROAMING THE COUNTRYSIDE, KICKING PEOPLE OUT OF THEIR HOMES. VICIOUS AND CRUEL.
BUT WITH VERY FESTIVE HAIR. METHINKS 'TIS SIMONE.

RAGNA DEMONS KEEP THEIR PREY ALIVE FOR THIRTY-SIX HOURS BEFORE FEEDING. SOMETHING ABOUT ADRENALINE BEING YUMMY. SO THERE'S TIME. BUT THERE'S TRAVEL, SO IF WE'RE GONNA GO, I'D CALL IT AN AY-SAP.

WE BRING NISHA BACK, SHE GIVES US INTEL ON SIMONE'S PLANS BEFORE SHE STRIKES AGAIN. A WIN WOULD BE NICE.
CAN YOU TWO HOLD DOWN THE FORT WHILE I GO WITH ANDREW?

ROAD TRIP! SWEET!
BUFF. YOU SURE ABOUT THIS? HOURS AND HOURS OF TRAVEL TIME WITH ANDREW? REALLY?
COME ON. HE'S MATURED. I CAN ABSOLUTELY HANDLE HIM.

...UNLESS THE CRYSTAL IN THE LIGHTSABER IS MADE OF KRYPTONITE, BECAUSE THEN, SURE, A JEDI COULD TOTALLY KICK SUPERMAN'S ASS...
...WHICH IS WHY I ALWAYS THOUGHT VANITY SMURF WAS KIND OF MISUNDERSTOOD...
...BUT THE WORST PART WAS THAT LEE GOT REALLY FAT, AND DUALLA WAS PROBABLY ALL, COME BACK, BILLY, BUT HE COULDN'T COME BACK, BECAUSE HE WAS DEAD, SO NOW SHE WAS STUCK WITH FAT LEE, AND THAT WAS NOT WHAT SHE SIGNED ON FOR, BELIEVE ME.
...IN HER PRISON CELL, READING ABOUT HOW FASCISTS TOOK OVER ENGLAND, AND THE WHOLE STORY IS ON TOILET PAPER, BUT IT'S NOT GROSS LIKE YOU WOULD THINK, IT'S BEAUTIFUL...
GILES WAS THE ONLY ONE WHO EVER HAD A CLERIC WITH HIGHER STRENGTH AND INTELLIGENCE THAN MY CLERIC, AND HEY, HAVE YOU TALKED TO HIM LATELY, WHAT'S GOING ON THERE?
... SO I SAY IF YOU HAVE TO DO ANOTHER MOVIE, FINE, I GET IT, BUT WHO CARES ABOUT AHNOLD, YOU GOTTA BRING BACK LINDA HAMILTON, THAT'S WHO PEOPLE WANT TO SEE...
SEE, THE IDEA IS THAT HELEN KELLER BECOMES LIKE A SECRET AGENT FOR THE GOVERNMENT, RIGHT? WHICH MAKES HER HELEN KILLER, GET IT? GENIUS!
...AND SOMETIMES I'M JUST SO MAD AT HEATH LEDGER, BUT JUST FOR A MINUTE, THEN I GET SAD AGAIN.
DO YOU THINK I SHOULD START DRESSING LIKE DON DRAPER, BECAUSE I THINK I COULD TOTALLY PULL IT OFF...
MY TEAM AND I SAVED THIS ITALIAN COUNT ONCE, AND HE WAS REALLY GRATEFUL, SAID I COULD BORROW HIS CAR WHENEVER I NEEDED IT, AND HE'S ALWAYS OFFERING TO GIVE ME PRIVATE DRIVING LESSONS, WHICH I DON'T NEED, 'CAUSE LOOK HOW FAST WE'RE GOING!
...AND DIDDY LOOKS AT ALL THE GUYS AND SAYS, IF YOU WANNA BE MAKING THE BAND, THEN NO BITCHASSNESS! ACTUALLY, I DON'T REALLY KNOW WHAT THAT MEANS...
...BUT WHY WOULD A JEDI BE FIGHTING SUPERMAN IN THE FIRST PLACE? THEY'RE ON THE SAME SIDE! DUH!
JEM IS TRULY OUTRAGEOUS, TRULY, TRULY, TRULY OUTRAGEOUS...
AND SUDDENLY DANIEL CRAIG IS MY NEW FAVORITE BOND, AND I NEVER THOUGHT THAT COULD EVER--
STOP.

YOU SAID DANIEL CRAIG. I LIKE DANIEL CRAIG. I GET DANIEL CRAIG. HE'S SO...
...GRITTY AND REAL?

UM, SURE. OH! AND THAT THING WHERE HE'S RUNNING ON ROOFTOPS AND CRANES? I'VE DONE THAT, AND I WAS STILL SCARED FOR HIM.
RIGHT! I KNOW! GRITTY, REAL, AND VULNERABLE!

AND THOSE SWIM TRUNKS. HELLO, DADDY.
YEAH, I HAVE NO OPINION ABOUT THOSE.

ANDREW, ARE WE GEEK-BONDING? YOU AND ME? WHO'D HAVE THUNK?
I KNOW. OOOH, WHAT ABOUT PIERCE BROSNAN? DID YOU LIKE HIM?
IN WHAT? MRS. DOUBTFIRE?
AUUUGGGH! HOW DARE YOU!!

THE READINGS SAY SHE'S THIS WAY.
TIMING'S ODD. SIMONE KICKING IT UP A NOTCH JUST AS THE WORLD STARTS GETTING SLAYERPHOBIC.

NOT REALLY. ONCE PEOPLE FOUND OUT ABOUT US, IT WAS AN OPPORTUNITY FOR HER. PEOPLE ARE MORE LIKELY TO BE AFRAID OF HER NOW.
SHE TAKES ADVANTAGE OF THEIR FEARS, SHE GETS WHAT SHE WANTS. SHE'S A BULLY. I'VE HAD SOME EXPERIENCE WITH BULLIES. GROWING UP.
YES. I SUPPOSE YOU DID.
THE LAIR SHOULD BE HERE. WE OUGHT TO BE SEEING IT ANY SECOND--
UM... IS THAT IT?

YEAH. THAT WOULD BE A RAGNA'S VERSION OF A WEB. IRON, STEEL. AND THE SNARE AT THE TOP TO TRAP AND SUSPEND HER PREY.
DELIGHTFUL. SO LET'S GO GET NISHA DOWN.

SHE ALIVE?
YES. SHE IS.
AND SHE'S KIND OF NOT HAPPY.
WELL, WELL, WELL. NISHA. I SEE WE'VE GOTTEN OURSELVES INTO QUITE A JAM.
I'M GONNA GET MY FOOT INTO QUITE YOUR ASS SOON AS I'M FREE, YOU TINY--
IS THAT SLANG FOR "THANKS, I APPRECIATE THE RESCUE"? YOU'RE WELCOME.
WHATEVER. JUST GET ME DOWN. THAT THING IS COMING BACK.
WHAT THING?
OH. THAT THING.
LOOKS LIKE CHARLOTTE'S HEADING BACK TO THE WEB. ANDREW, HELP ME GET NISHA DOWN BEFORE THAT THING GETS UP HERE.
YOU LOSERS WOULDN'T HAVE TO GET ME DOWN IF YOU HADN'T CREATED THIS MESS IN THE FIRST PLACE.
HEY! A LITTLE GRATITUDE WOULD NOT BE OUT OF ORDER.
IF NOT FOR ANDREW BEING ON TOP OF THINGS AND MONITORING THE DEMON SITUATION, YOU GET EATEN. IT'S NOT OUR FAULT YOU FELL INTO A--WHAT--A MANGA TRAP OR WHATEVER.
PLEASE. YOU SERIOUSLY BELIEVE THAT? RAGNA DEMONS DIED OUT IN THE ELEVENTH CENTURY.
BUT SOMEONE SPENT ALL HIS FREE TIME IN ITALY PERFORMING RECOMBINANT D.N.A. EXPERIMENTS TO BREED THEM BACK INTO EXISTENCE. GUESS WHO?

CLICK

WHRRRRR...

SO... I'M THINKING, DOES IT REALLY MATTER *HOW* WE GOT NISHA IN CUSTODY?
WE GOT HER, LET'S JUST GET HER BACK TO HEADQUARTERS, HERE WE GO...
YOU BRED A DANGEROUS DEMON, AND LIED TO ME ABOUT IT. I THINK IT'S SALIENT, YES.
THUNK

I DIDN'T LIE! I SAID NISHA WAS IN A RAGNA TRAP. I DIDN'T SAY WHERE IT CAME FROM.
I'M FINE, BY THE WAY.

CRRAACCK!
NNNNH!
BUFFY!

YOU ALL RIGHT, NISH? WE GOT HERE AS SOON AS WE TRACKED YOU.
FINE. BIT OF A HEAD RUSH. BEEN UPSIDE DOWN FOR EIGHTEEN HOURS.
WAK
AND YOU. NOT NICE, CAPTURING ONE OF MY GIRLS, BUFF. LUCKILY, I GOT A REAL SKILLED WICCAN WHO WAS STRONG ENOUGH TO BEAM ONE PERSON RIGHT HERE TO THE SIGNAL.
"BEAMING," RIGHT, ANDREW? THAT'S WHAT YOU STARGATE NERDS CALL IT?
IT'S STAR TREK, HAG. WERE YOU NOT LISTENING TO ANY OF MY LECTURES?
NICE ENTRANCE. LOOK, SLAPPY-FIGHT'S OVER, SIMONE. COME BACK WITH US BEFORE THAT SPIDER THING GETS UP HERE. WE CAN SORT OUT WHATEVER'S--
COME BACK?! HAVEN'T YOU HEARD? WE'RE THE BAD GUYS NOW. PEOPLE THINK VAMPS ARE COOL AND SLAYERS ARE THE THREAT.
DIFFERENCE BETWEEN YOU AND ME?
I AM A THREAT.
COME ON, SIMONE, YOU REALLY THINK A GUN IS THE WAY TO DEAL WITH ME?
WHAT? THIS? PLEASE. I'M NOT HERE TO SHOOT YOU. AND IF I WAS, I'D USE A REAL GUN, NOT ONE OF THESE TOYS. GUNS I LIKE. BUT THIS? THIS ISN'T FOR YOU.
IT'S FOR HER.
PFFFFFFZZT

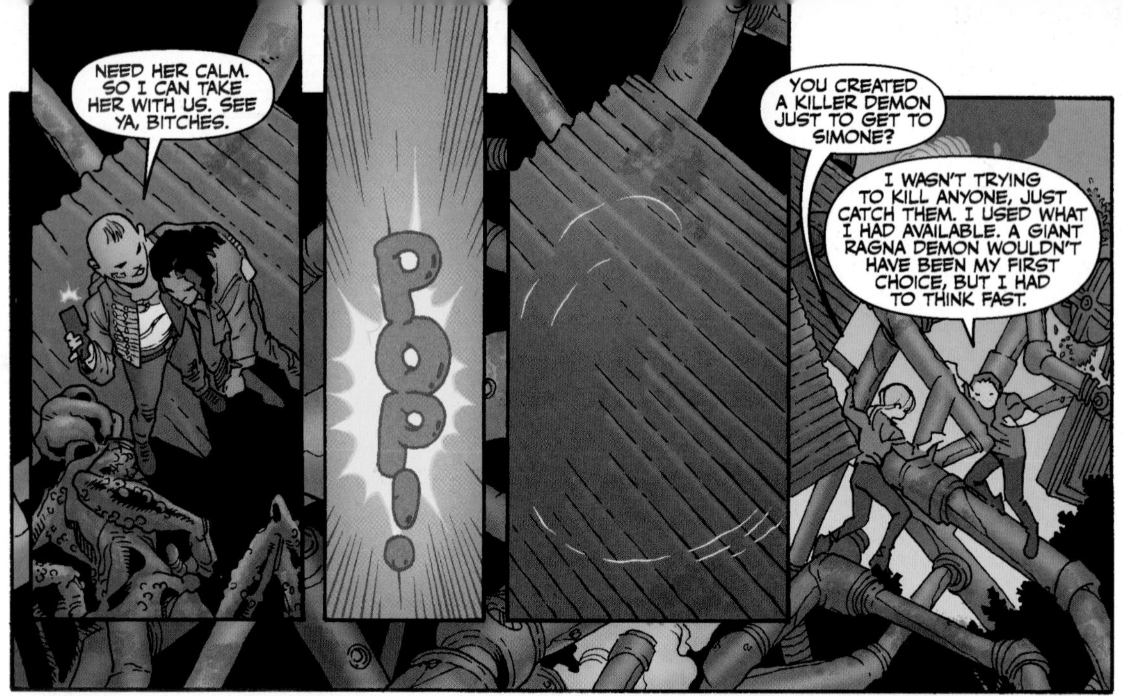
NEED HER CALM. SO I CAN TAKE HER WITH US. SEE YA, BITCHES.
POP!
YOU CREATED A KILLER DEMON JUST TO GET TO SIMONE?
I WASN'T TRYING TO KILL ANYONE, JUST CATCH THEM. I USED WHAT I HAD AVAILABLE. A GIANT RAGNA DEMON WOULDN'T HAVE BEEN MY FIRST CHOICE, BUT I HAD TO THINK FAST.

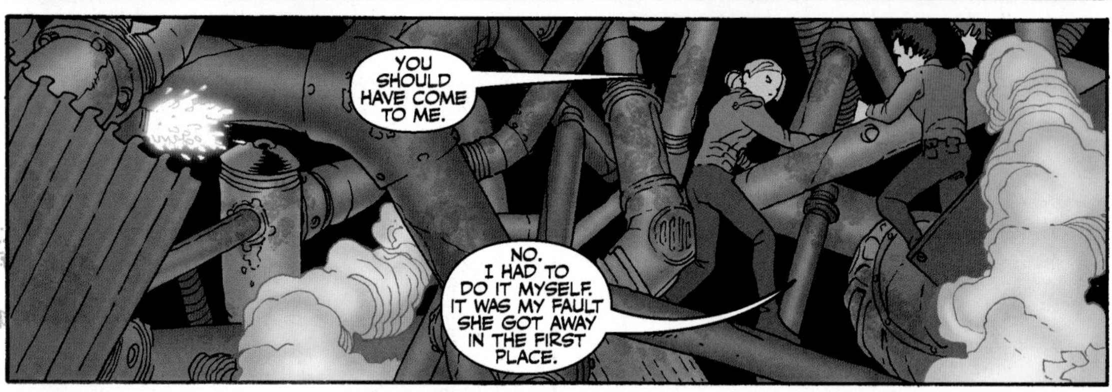
YOU SHOULD HAVE COME TO ME.
NO. I HAD TO DO IT MYSELF. IT WAS MY FAULT SHE GOT AWAY IN THE FIRST PLACE.

SIMONE WASN'T YOUR FAULT. RONA WAS THE ONE WHO--
I WAS SIMONE'S WATCHER. MAYBE YOU DON'T BLAME ME FOR HER GOING BAD. BUT I BLAME MYSELF. AND I HAD TO PROVE MYSELF.
WE BOTH KNOW HOW FAR I'VE COME SINCE I MET YOU. I FEEL LIKE I'VE EARNED YOUR TRUST. YOURS AND XANDER'S AND WILLOW'S. THIS WHOLE ORGANIZATION.

YOU *HAVE.*
AND THAT'S WHY I'M SCARED.

I'VE NEVER HAD THIS BEFORE. WITH ANYONE. NOW THAT I KNOW WHAT IT FEELS LIKE... I DIDN'T WANT IT TO GET TAKEN AWAY. WHAT IF YOU ENDED UP BLAMING ME FOR THIS SOMEDAY?
I WOULDN'T.
BUT I HAD TO MAKE SURE. I DIDN'T WANT YOU TO LOSE FAITH IN ME. SO I TRIED TO FIX IT.

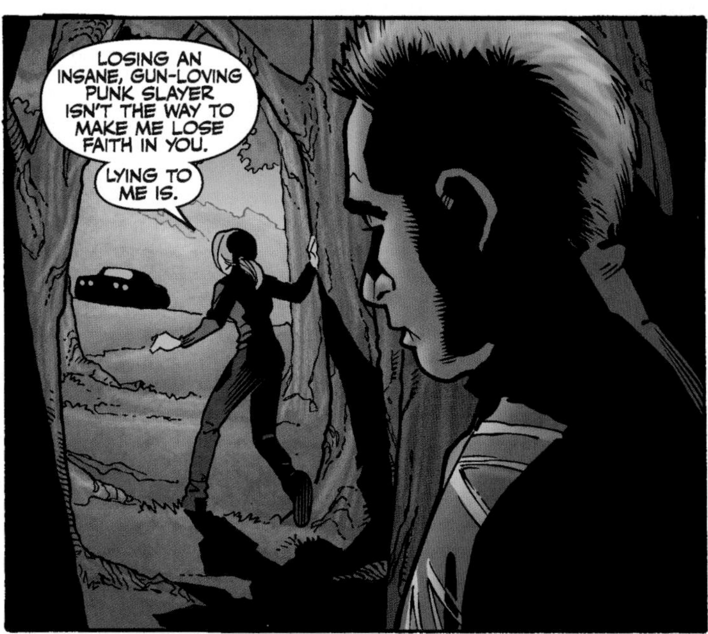
LOSING AN INSANE, GUN-LOVING PUNK SLAYER ISN'T THE WAY TO MAKE ME LOSE FAITH IN YOU.
LYING TO ME IS.

SIMONE HAS THE RAGNA NOW. IF I KNOW HER, SHE'LL USE IT AGAINST PEOPLE. CIVILIANS.
CAN YOU TRACK IT?

I EQUIPPED THE DEMON WITH SOME GENETIC MODIFICATIONS. RADIOACTIVE ISOTOPES. WE CAN TRACK THEM.
IRONIC, RIGHT? ALL THE WORK I PUT INTO BREEDING THIS DEMON IS WHAT MADE YOU MAD, BUT IT'S ALSO THE THING THAT WILL HELP US FIND IT, SO, IF YOU THINK ABOUT IT, YAY, AND, ALSO, HMM, YOU DON'T SEEM TO BE A FAN OF IRONY, SO, YEAH...
IT'S ON AN ISLAND OFF THE COAST.
GOOD. LET'S GO.

IT'S BEAUTIFUL.
WE SHOULD TOTALLY BRING THE GIRLS HERE FOR A VACATION SOME DAY.
I MEAN, AFTER WE GET RID OF THE EVIL SLAYERS AND THE KILLER SPIDER DEMON. OBVIES. ARE YOU STILL MAD AT ME?
EXCUSE ME. YOU'RE NOT SUPPOSED TO GO IN THERE.
NO ONE IS SUPPOSED TO GO IN THERE.
YOU SPEAK ENGLISH.

MY GRANDMOTHER YELLED AT HER. AND THE ANGRY WOMAN HURT MY GRANDMOTHER.
WHERE DID EVERYONE GO?
MOST FLED TO THE MAINLAND. BUT MY GRANDMOTHER AND I, WE HAVE NOTHING THERE. SO WE STAYED HERE. ON THE DOCKS. WE DON'T GO INTO THE VILLAGE.

LOOKS LIKE SIMONE'S MADE HERSELF COMFORTABLE HERE.

VILLA

SIGNAL'S COMING FROM THIS PLACE. THE OPERA HOUSE.

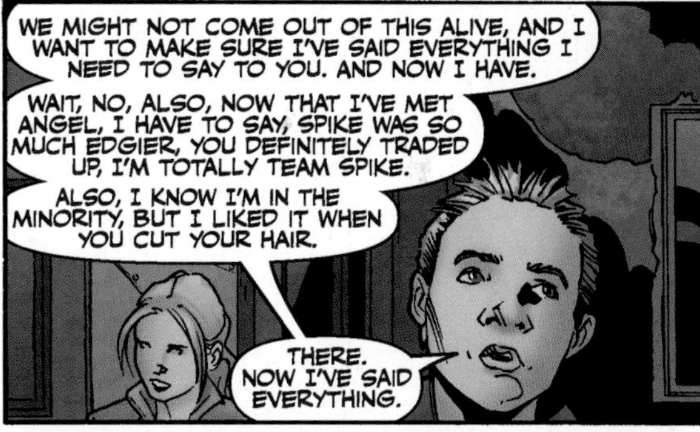

IF WE'RE GONNA FIND THIS THING, WE'LL NEED SOME--
--LIGHTS.
NICE OF YOU TO MAKE IT. SOME OF THE GIRLS WERE GETTING CONCERNED ABOUT YOU. BUT I TOLD THEM NOTHING WOULD STOP THE GREAT AND POWERFUL BUFFY FROM RIDING UP ON HER GREAT STEED. OR, AS THE CASE MAY BE, HER PATHETIC LAP DOG.
I KNEW YOU COULDN'T RESIST FOLLOWING ME. COUNTING ON IT, REALLY. BECAUSE HERE...
...I'VE GOT MY MUSCLE WITH ME.

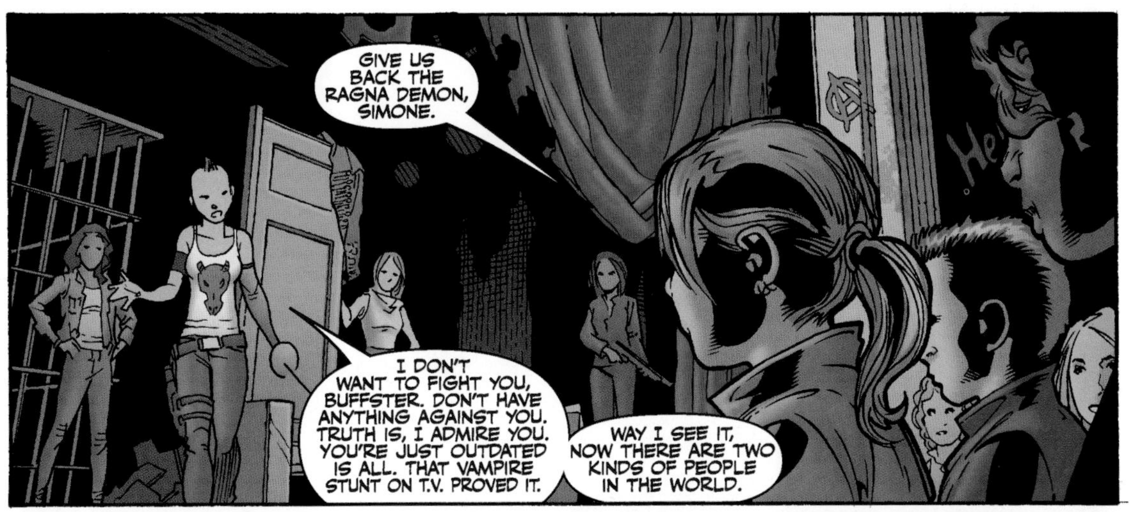
GIVE US BACK THE RAGNA DEMON, SIMONE.
I DON'T WANT TO FIGHT YOU, BUFFSTER. DON'T HAVE ANYTHING AGAINST YOU. TRUTH IS, I ADMIRE YOU. YOU'RE JUST OUTDATED IS ALL. THAT VAMPIRE STUNT ON T.V. PROVED IT.
WAY I SEE IT, NOW THERE ARE TWO KINDS OF PEOPLE IN THE WORLD.

THE ONES WHO FEAR US SO MUCH, THEY HOPE SOMEONE KILLS US ALL...
AND THE ONES SO STUPID, THEY WANT TO BE THE ONES TO TRY.
I DON'T HAVE MUCH USE FOR EITHER.
SO YOU THINK THE ANSWER IS TO TAKE OVER AN ISLAND.

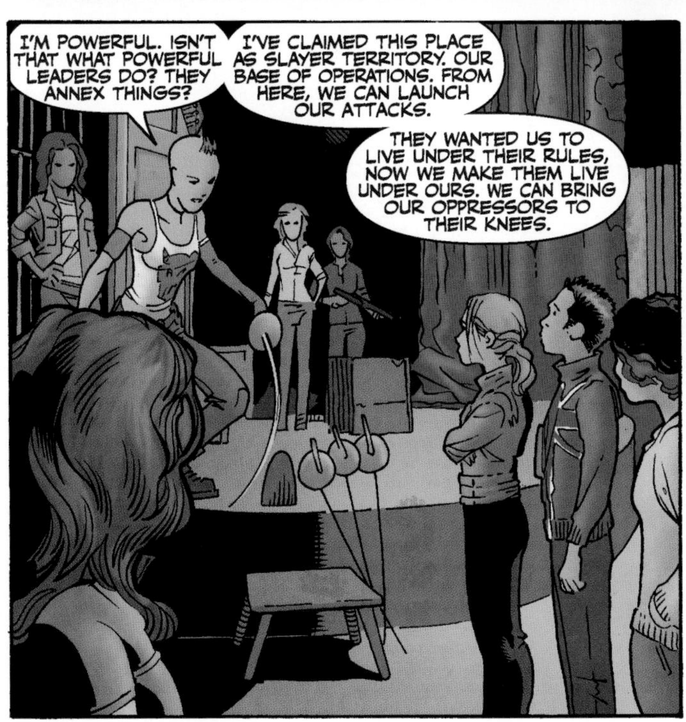
I'M POWERFUL. ISN'T THAT WHAT POWERFUL LEADERS DO? THEY ANNEX THINGS?
I'VE CLAIMED THIS PLACE AS SLAYER TERRITORY. OUR BASE OF OPERATIONS. FROM HERE, WE CAN LAUNCH OUR ATTACKS.
THEY WANTED US TO LIVE UNDER THEIR RULES, NOW WE MAKE THEM LIVE UNDER OURS. WE CAN BRING OUR OPPRESSORS TO THEIR KNEES.

WE CAN BE THE AGENTS OF CHANGE AND FEAR WE WERE MEANT TO BE. *IT'S WHO WE ARE.*
IT'S NOT WHO *I* AM.
YOU KNOW I'M RIGHT. AND GUESS WHAT? ANDREW'S LITTLE SPIDER FRIEND CAN HELP. BREED A FEW MORE, WE GOT OURSELVES A WEAPON, EVERYONE FALLS INTO LINE.

JUST GIVE ME ANDREW.

WHAT??!?!

YOU'D GIVE BACK THE DEMON... FOR JUST... ***ANDREW?***

NO OFFENSE.

NONE TAKEN.

YES. COME ON! SOMEONE LIKE ***HIM?*** WAS IN CHARGE OF SOMEONE LIKE ***ME?*** IN CASE YOU HAVEN'T FIGURED IT OUT, I'M NOT A FAN OF AUTHORITY TO BEGIN WITH. AND HE'S KIND OF A DRILL SERGEANT, WHICH, YOU KNOW... PISS OFF. I WANT MY PAYBACK. ALSO, HE'S INCREDIBLY ANNOYING.

YEAH, WELL, THAT PART YOU GET USED TO.

BUT YOU'RE NOT TAKING HIM.

HEYMMMMMPHH!

DOES THAT FEEL PRECARIOUS? IT LOOKS PRECARIOUS. AND IT LOOKS LIKE YOU'RE TRAPPED.
SIMONE! WATCH OUT!
SMASHHHH!
I'VE BEEN DOING THIS LONGER THAN YOU. WHICH MEANS I'M MORE EXPERIENCED, SO YOU'RE DONE.
AND I'M YOUNGER THAN YOU. WHICH MEANS I'M FASTER, SO YOU'RE F*@%ED.
THIS ONE IS A REAL GUN.

I'M REALLY NOT A FAN OF GUNS.
AND HERE I THOUGHT WE HAD SO MUCH IN COMMON, PHILOSOPHY-WISE.
THIS IS STILL SO EASY. JUST GIVE ME THE LOSER. YOU GET THE DEMON. NO ONE HAS TO GET HURT. WELL...

ALMOST NO ONE.
NO.
BUFFY...
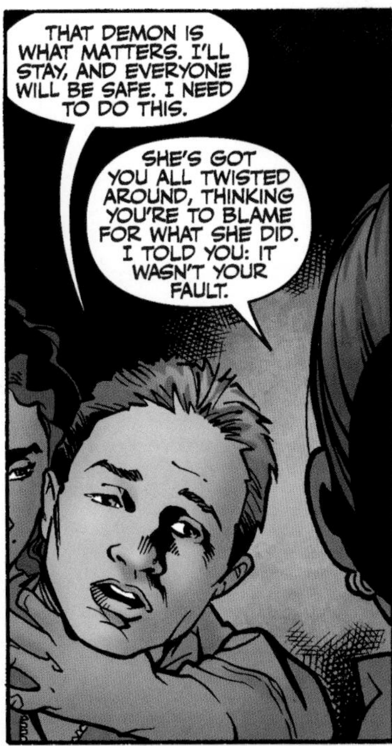
THAT DEMON IS WHAT MATTERS. I'LL STAY, AND EVERYONE WILL BE SAFE. I NEED TO DO THIS.
SHE'S GOT YOU ALL TWISTED AROUND, THINKING YOU'RE TO BLAME FOR WHAT SHE DID. I TOLD YOU: IT WASN'T YOUR FAULT.

I'M NOT TWISTED AROUND. IT'S SIMPLE LOGIC. SHE'LL HURT COUNTLESS PEOPLE WITH THE DEMON. I'M JUST ONE. THE NEEDS OF THE MANY OUTWEIGH THE NEEDS--
ANDREW.
I'VE BEEN HANGING OUT WITH XANDER FOR EIGHT YEARS. I'VE GEEK-BONDED WITH HIM, TOO, AND I'M FAMILIAR WITH THE BOOK OF NERD QUOTES. I'M NOT MOVED.

SIMONE? KEEP THE DEMON, DON'T KEEP THE DEMON. I DON'T CARE. I'LL FIND A WAY TO STOP YOU. BUT ANDREW COMES WITH ME. I DON'T WALK AWAY FROM MY PEOPLE.
BECAUSE THAT'S WHO *I* AM.

THAT'S A SHAME. SEE...
IT'S MY SIXTEEN SLAYERS TO YOUR *ONE*.
I THINK YOU MISCALCULATED, SIMONE.

ITALY SQUAD! IT'S ITALY SQUAD!
MR. HARRIS SAID MR. WELLS WAS GOING TO ENGAGE SIMONE, AND WE WEREN'T ABOUT TO LET HIM DO THAT ALONE. HE'S OUR WATCHER. WHERE HE GOES, WE GO.

MR. WELLS COMES WITH US.
UM, I'M ACTUALLY HERE, TOO.
...AND BUFFY ALSO COMES WITH US.

GOOD WORK. IF WE NEED TO FIGHT 'EM TO GET BACK CONTROL OF THE ISLAND, WE CAN--
MA'AM. I DON'T THINK THAT'S A GOOD IDEA. EVEN WITH THE NUMBERS ON OUR SIDE, THERE ARE STILL WEAPONS AT PLAY. IF JUST ONE OF SIMONE'S PEOPLE BREAKS FREE, WE GET A FIREFIGHT.

I PROMISED I'D GET THE VILLAGERS BACK THEIR HOME.
ALL DUE RESPECT, MA'AM. I SUGGEST WE GET THE REMAINING VILLAGERS TO THE MAINLAND AND LIVE TO FIGHT SIMONE ANOTHER DAY.

FINE. YOU CAN KEEP THE ISLAND.

NOW GIVE ME BACK MY NERD.

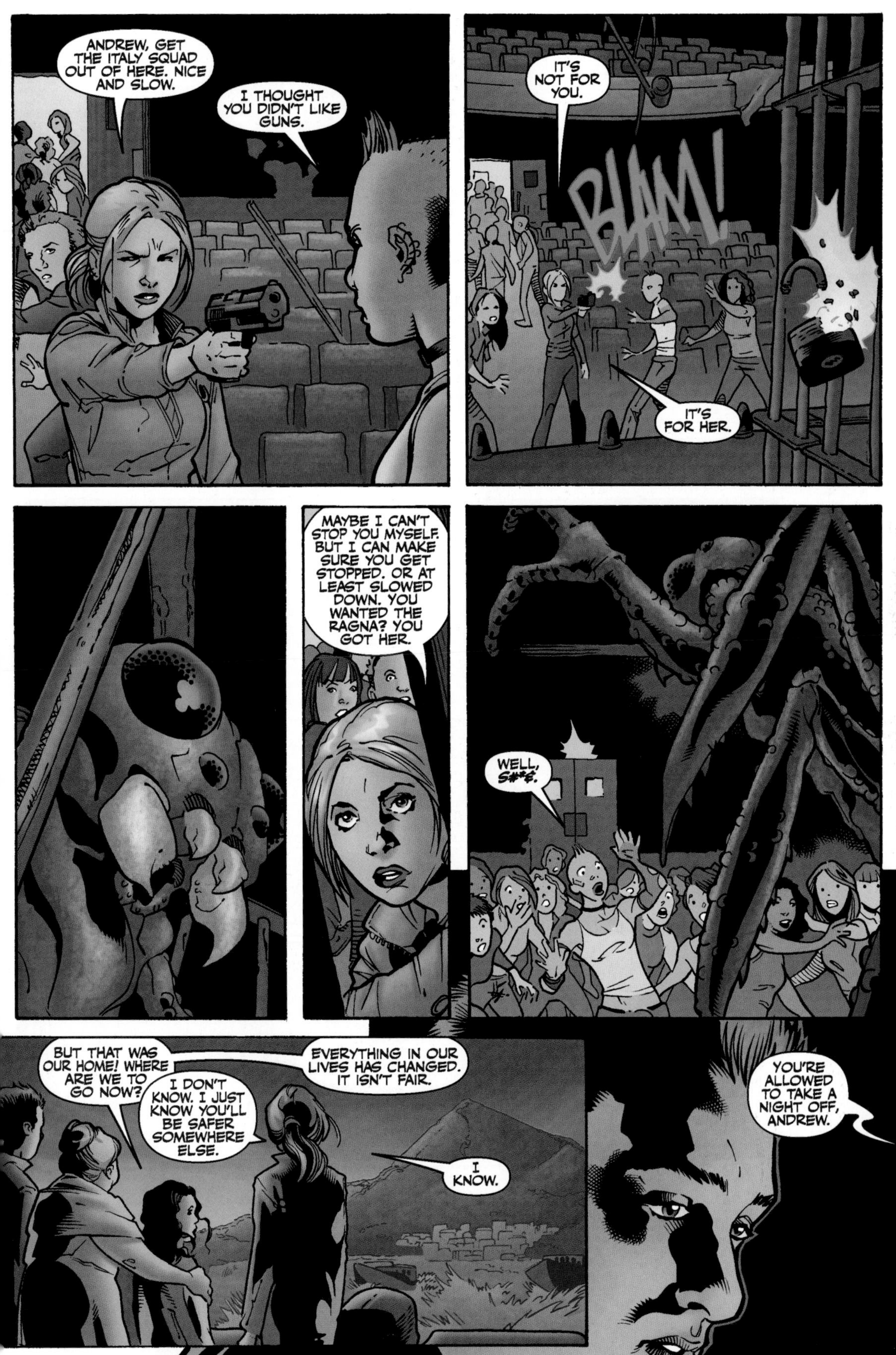

ANDREW, GET THE ITALY SQUAD OUT OF HERE. NICE AND SLOW.
I THOUGHT YOU DIDN'T LIKE GUNS.
IT'S NOT FOR YOU.
BLAM!
IT'S FOR HER.
MAYBE I CAN'T STOP YOU MYSELF. BUT I CAN MAKE SURE YOU GET STOPPED. OR AT LEAST SLOWED DOWN. YOU WANTED THE RAGNA? YOU GOT HER.
WELL, S#*$.
BUT THAT WAS OUR HOME! WHERE ARE WE TO GO NOW?
I DON'T KNOW. I JUST KNOW YOU'LL BE SAFER SOMEWHERE ELSE.
EVERYTHING IN OUR LIVES HAS CHANGED. IT ISN'T FAIR.
I KNOW.
YOU'RE ALLOWED TO TAKE A NIGHT OFF, ANDREW.

I'M JUST COLLECTING ALL MY INFORMATION ABOUT THE RAGNA. IF WE'RE EVER FORCED TO FIGHT HER, I WANT US TO KNOW ALL HER WEAKNESSES.
I'M SURE SIMONE AND HER CREW TOOK CARE OF HER, WHICH IS... TRULY NON-COMFORTING.

LOOK, ANDREW. YOU WERE WILLING TO SACRIFICE YOURSELF TO SAVE INNOCENT PEOPLE. FOR A GREATER GOOD. THAT'S HUGE FOR YOU. YOU SHOULD BE PROUD.
BUT YOU WERE RIGHT. I LIED TO YOU.

YEAH, YOU'RE PART OF THE FAMILY. GET USED TO SCREWING UP FOR GOOD REASONS, IT'S WHAT WE DO. SWING BY WHEN YOU'VE GOT THE SPECS WRITTEN UP. WE'LL TAKE A LOOK.

I'M PART OF THE FAMILY?

The End

SAFE

UM... SORRY?
SORRY! I QUIT! I GIVE--
I NEVER EVEN WANTED TO BE CHOSEN!
I'M NOT GOING TO HURT YOU. I JUST WANT TO SUCK ON YOU FOR A WHILE.
HAVEN'T YOU HEARD?
EVERYONE WANTS TO BE A VAMPIRE N...
...OW.
MAN, THEY ALWAYS GOTTA BE SO CHATTY.
OH, MY GOD! YOU'RE HER!
YOU'RE BUFFY!
BAKER

SHE'S CALLING ME NAMES, G.
SHE'S *CONFUSED,* FAITH. THAT'S THE POINT.
ARE YOU GUYS HERE TO TRAIN ME?
WE'RE CHECKING UP. YOU BAILED ON YOUR SQUAD.
THEY WEREN'T DOING ANYTHING! I WANTED TO GET IN THE FIELD! I'M READY!
...WHY ARE YOU SCARED OF *ME* NOW?
AHH!
KOFF KOFF
GROSS...
FIRST THING SHE'S GOT TO LEARN, G., IS NOT TO KEEP HER MOUTH OPEN WHEN SHE SLAYS.

THANKS. I'LL REMEMBER THAT.
LOOKS LIKE I'M NOT READY FOR "SLAYER SANCTUARY" YET.
SLAYER SANCTUARY?
YEAH. FOR SLAYERS THAT DON'T WANT TO BE...YOU KNOW...
WE GET TO CHOOSE WHETHER WE WANT TO BE CHOSEN OR NOT.
MY NAME'S COURTNEY. CORT'S OKAY. BUT DON'T CALL ME COCO. MY SISTER DOES--I HATE THAT.
SO YOU'RE FAITH? I'VE HEARD ABOUT *YOU*, TOO.
YAY. LET'S BOND.
TELL ME MORE ABOUT THIS SLAYER SANCTUARY.

YOU'VE NEVER HEARD OF SLAYER SANCTUARY?
SOME OF THE CHOSEN FROM A BUNCH OF SQUADS HAVE GONE.
WE NEED TO FIND THIS PLACE.
THAT MAKES YOU GUIDE DOG.
AWESOME.
DON'T CALL ME A DOG.
LATER.
WE JUST MADE IT. THIS IS THE ONLY TRAIN THAT REACHES HANSELSTADT. IT'S DEEP IN THE MOUNTAINS.
YEAH, SO TELL ME HOWCUM THE SLAYERS HAVE A SANCTUARY...
"...IN THE MIDDLE OF A DRACULA FLICK?"
IF THESE GIRLS ARE HIDING HERE, SEEING YOU MIGHT GET THEM BACK IN THE FIGHT.
WE'RE NOT RECRUITING, GILES. I KNOW THINGS ARE WORSE OUT THERE, BUT IF THESE GIRLS WANT TO SIT IT OUT, THAT'S THEIR CALL.
LOOK OUT THE WINDOW.

VAMPIRES. I DON'T UNDERSTAND. WHAT ARE THEY WAITING FOR?
THEY'RE NOT ALLOWED IN HANSELSTADT.
THERE IT IS. THE TOWN.
I THINK MR. GILES IS RIGHT. IF ALL THE CHOSEN WHO WERE IN HIDING SAW YOU, FAITH, SAW WHAT YOU COULD DO, HOW YOU'VE INSPIRED ME, THEY WOULD REJOIN THE WAR.
THEY'D CHOOSE TO BE CHOSEN AGAIN.
I'VE INSPIRED YOU? THAT'S A FIRST.
YOU'RE TOO HARD ON YOURSELF, FAITH.

RUPERT GILES.
DUNCAN FILLWORTHE? YOU'RE HERE?
WERE YOU EXPECTING US?
I TRY TO MEET EVERY TRAIN THAT COMES INTO TOWN. I'M VERY GLAD TO SEE YOU ARE SAFE.
IT'S NOT A PLEASANT TIME FOR WATCHER OR SLAYER.
SOON.
YES, RUPERT, BUT THERE ARE ALTERNATIVES TO RUNNING SCARED.
HANSELSTADT FOR ONE. THE VAMPIRES KNOW IF THEY COME IN...
...WE HAVE AN ARMY OF SLAYERS TO FACE THEM. WHO'LL LEAVE THEM ALONE IF THEY STAY OUT.
A STALEMATE. NOT EXACTLY A LASTING SOLUTION.
WHERE ARE THE GIRLS?

I ADMIT, I WANTED TO KNOW YOUR INTENT BEFORE WE TOOK YOU TO THEM.
THIS *TOWN* IS MY RESPONSIBILITY, AS ARE *THEY.*
BUT YOU CAN MEET THEM WHEN YOU'VE EATEN.
AND IF THEY DECIDE TO LEAVE, TO JOIN THE COMING BATTLE?
WHY PROTECT A HUMANITY THAT NOW HATES AND FEARS YOU, AND RESENTS THAT YOU EVER TRIED TO SAVE THEM FROM VAMPIRES AND DEMONS?
YOU KNOW, YOU SOUND SO MUCH LIKE I USED TO.
I'M STARTING TO FEEL AT HOME...
...WHICH I LEFT THE FIRST CHANCE I GOT.
I THINK IT'S TIME, THEN, FOR YOU TO JOIN THE OTHER SLAYERS. THEY'RE WAITING FOR YOU IN THE TOWN LIBRARY.
GO AHEAD, FAITH. TAKE COURTNEY WITH YOU.

BÄKEREI
YOU NOTICE THERE AREN'T ANY KIDS ANYWHERE.
OTHEK
YES, THAT'S WHY WE'RE GRATEFUL THAT YOU SLAYERS CAME HERE. WHY WE'RE GRATEFUL THE COUNCIL TOOK AN INTEREST IN OUR TOWN.
WHAT IS IT WITH WATCHERS AND KEEPING SLAYERS IN LIBRARIES?
THIS REALLY OBVIOUS TRAP FEELS LIKE A TRAP.
SO WHAT DO WE DO?

I'M TIRED OF BEATING AROUND THE BUSH.
'SIDES, THESE HOKEY OLD STIFFS...
...THEY GONNA COME UP WITH SOMETHING I AIN'T SEEN?
NO...
SOMETHING YOU HAVE.
THE THIRD...
DO YOU HAVE ANY IDEA, GIRL, HOW MANY I'VE KILLED SINCE YOUR FIRST FEW STEPS AS A SLAYER?
HOW MANY I'VE SIRED SINCE?
HOW MANY THEY HAVE SIRED THEMSELVES?

KEEP AWAY FROM ME!
SHE'S A SLAYER.
NEW ONE. STILL GOT THE SMELL ON HER.
LET'S SEE IF SHE TASTES--
PAFT
PAFT
AH!
DON'T MATTER WHAT PEOPLE SAY... THAT AIN'T THE WAY TO A MAN'S HEART.
WELL HELL, TWO OUT OF THREE AIN'T BAD.

YOU COULD HAVE FOLLOWED, FAITH. YOU COULD HAVE STOPPED ME. YOU REEK OF FAILURE AND LAZINESS, AND IT'S DELICIOUS...
...DELICIOUS AS ALL YOUR FRIENDS WERE.
SHUT UP!
WHAT'S GOING ON, FAITH?!
WHO ARE YOU SCREAMING AT?!
I'LL ANSWER YOUR SLAYER-IN-TRAINING QUESTIONS LATER! GOT A VAMP TO SNUFF!
I'M GOING TO SIRE YOU, FAITH.
AND THEN LET THE LITTLE GIRL KILL YOU. BE A BETTER SLAYER THAN YOU EVER WERE.
STOP THIS, FAITH! PLEASE! THERE'S NOTHING THERE!
THERE ARE NO VAMPIRES HERE!

EVERY DAY YOU HELP A SLAYER HIDE...
OR LEARN HOW TO HIDE YOURSELF, THE VAMPIRES BECOME STRONGER.
AS LONG AS VAMPIRES KNOW THIS IS A SANCTUARY FOR SLAYERS, THEY WON'T BOTHER US.
EVEN IF THERE ARE STILL SOME OUT THERE THAT WANT VENGEANCE AGAINST THE TWO REMAINING MEMBERS OF THE COUNCIL.
DO YOU KNOW FOR CERTAIN THAT WE ARE ALL THAT'S LEFT OF THE COUNCIL?

AND FORGIVE ME IF I DON'T SHARE YOUR BELIEF THAT THE VAMPIRES WILL STAY AWAY JUST BECAUSE THIS PLACE IS BRANDED A SAFE ZONE.
THEY'RE WAITING JUST OUTSIDE THIS TOWN. THEY'RE WAITING.

THERE WAS A DEMON THAT LIVED HERE, RUPERT. DID YOU KNOW THAT?

A DEMON? IS THAT WHAT THEY'RE AFRAID OF?

BEFORE I CAME TO HANSELSTADT, IT WAS FEEDING ON THE CHILDREN--UPON THE EXPRESSION OF THEIR FEARS AND REGRETS.

YOU SEE, CHILDREN DO NOT HAVE THE COPING MECHANISMS OF INTERNALIZING THEIR PROBLEMS AND SMILING THROUGH PAIN. CHILDREN ARE PURE NEED...
...NOT UNLIKE VAMPIRES.

FAITH!
TALK TO ME! WHAT'S GOING ON?!
WHO'S THERE?
OH MY GOD...

FAITH?
OH--!
MOM... DAD...?
WHAT ARE YOU DOING HERE?
YOU'RE TOGETHER?
BUT YOU HATE EACH OTHER.
BUT WE LOVE YOU. AND CAN'T DO THAT VERY WELL IF WE DON'T LOVE EACH OTHER. RIGHT?
OH DADDY, I THOUGHT IT WAS MY FAULT, FOR WHAT I SAID TO MOM, FOR WHAT I SAW...
IT FEELS SO GOOD TO HAVE YOUR ARMS AROUND ME AGAIN.

HAVE YOU EVER THOUGHT, RUPERT, ABOUT WHAT IT MUST BE LIKE TO BE A VAMPIRE?

I DON'T THINK I QUITE UNDERSTAND YOU.

THE VAMPIRE IS REGRET PERSONIFIED. A HUNGER FOR LIFE THAT'S BEEN DAMNED TO NEVER BE SATISFIED.

THAT IS WHY VAMPIRES WILL NEVER COME HERE. THE DEMON FEEDS ON THE MOST PRIMAL NEEDS AND FEARS. IT IS WHAT KEEPS US SAFE. THE ONLY TROUBLE IS...

...WELL, THESE FINE TOWNSPEOPLE RAN OUT OF CHILDREN.

...THEIR OWN CHILDREN...
SO... SO YOU SUPPLIED GIRLS... THE CHOSEN. SO THE DEMON WOULD KEEP THE VAMPIRES AWAY.
YOU LET WORD GET OUT OF A SLAYER'S SANCTUARY. TO...ATTRACT THEM. YOU...THIS IS VENGEANCE FOR YOU, ISN'T IT, DUNCAN?
REMEMBER WHO YOU WERE, RUPERT. A WATCHER. YOU'VE ALWAYS SENT SLAYERS TO THEIR DEATHS.
I'VE SAVED THE LIVES OF EVERYONE IN THIS TOWN.
YOU'RE WELCOME TO STAY, RUPERT.
THIS IS MADNESS.
YOU WEREN'T HERE.
THE VAMPIRES SLAUGHTERED US! EVERY ONE! AND FOR WHAT?!
FOR GIVING COUNSEL TO THE GIRLS THAT REJECTED US!
YOUR BUFFY! THINK OF WHAT SHE'S DONE TO YOU!
I REMEMBER WHEN THE TEACHER DIED. THE ONE YOU LOVED. SHE DIED BECAUSE BUFFY IGNORED YOU AND LOVED A VAMPIRE.
JENNY CALENDAR?

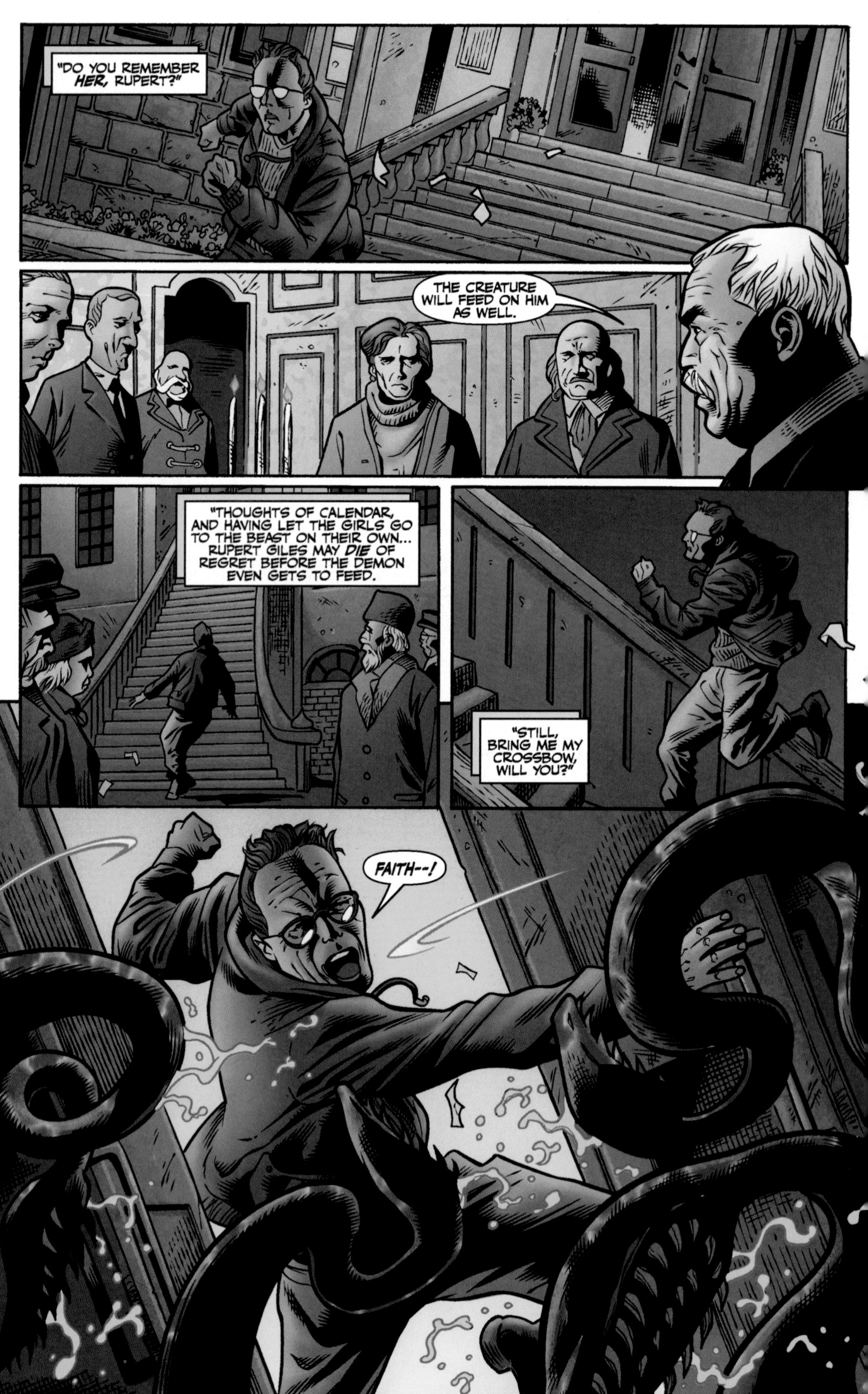
"DO YOU REMEMBER HER, RUPERT?"
THE CREATURE WILL FEED ON HIM AS WELL.
"THOUGHTS OF CALENDAR, AND HAVING LET THE GIRLS GO TO THE BEAST ON THEIR OWN... RUPERT GILES MAY DIE OF REGRET BEFORE THE DEMON EVEN GETS TO FEED.
"STILL, BRING ME MY CROSSBOW, WILL YOU?"
FAITH--!

COURTNEY!
I'M SORRY, MOM. I DIDN'T MEAN TO RUIN EVERYTHING.
LET IT HAVE HER, RUPERT. WALK AWAY.
IF IT DIES, THE TOWN WILL BE IN DANGER. THE VAMPIRES HAVE BEEN WAITING FOR ONE OF THE SLAYERS TO KILL THE DEMON. DON'T HELP THEM!
WHAT IS THE LOSS IF A FEW DISILLUSIONED SLAYERS HAVE TO BE SACRIFICED FOR THE LIVES IN THIS TOWN?
YOU'RE GOING TO REGRET THIS, DUNCAN.

I REGRET NOTHING. THAT'S WHY I'M STILL ALIVE.
NO!
HELP ME!
RUPERT?! FOR GOD'S SAKE, YOU'RE A WATCHER!
RUPERT! HELP ME! I'M SORRY!
NO... I DIDN'T MEAN... I'M NOT SORR... I...

THAT WAS YOUR LAST MEAL, OCTOBITCH.
EEAALLGGHH
CHOKE ON IT.

WHAT ARE THE ODDS THEY'VE COME TO PRAISE US?
WHAT DO WE DO NOW?
THE VAMPIRES WON'T BE AFRAID TO COME HERE NOW.
THAT'S NOT OUR PROBLEM. YOU'RE MURDERERS! YOU DESERVE TO DIE!
PROBABLY.
BUT WE'RE SLAYERS, AND WE DON'T LET PEOPLE DIE. NOT EVEN CRAPPY ONES.
YOU PEOPLE WANNA LIVE?
BACKEREY
THEN YOU FIGHT.
FAITH, I'M JUST...I HAVEN'T TRAINED...
THERE'S ONLY ONE LESSON, KID.
AIM FOR THE HEART.
The End

LIVING DOLL

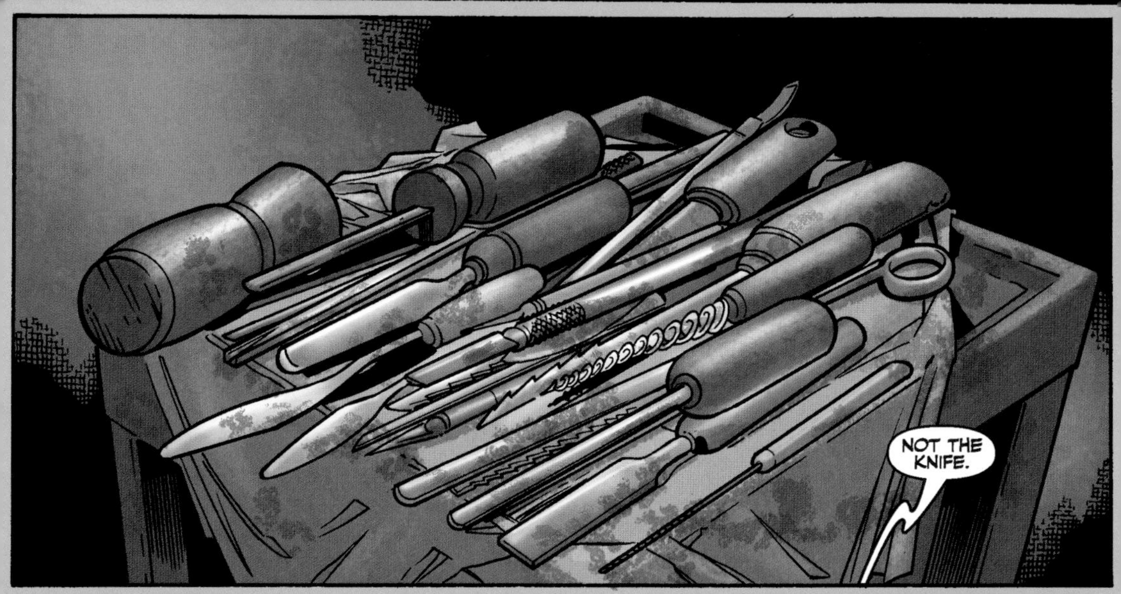

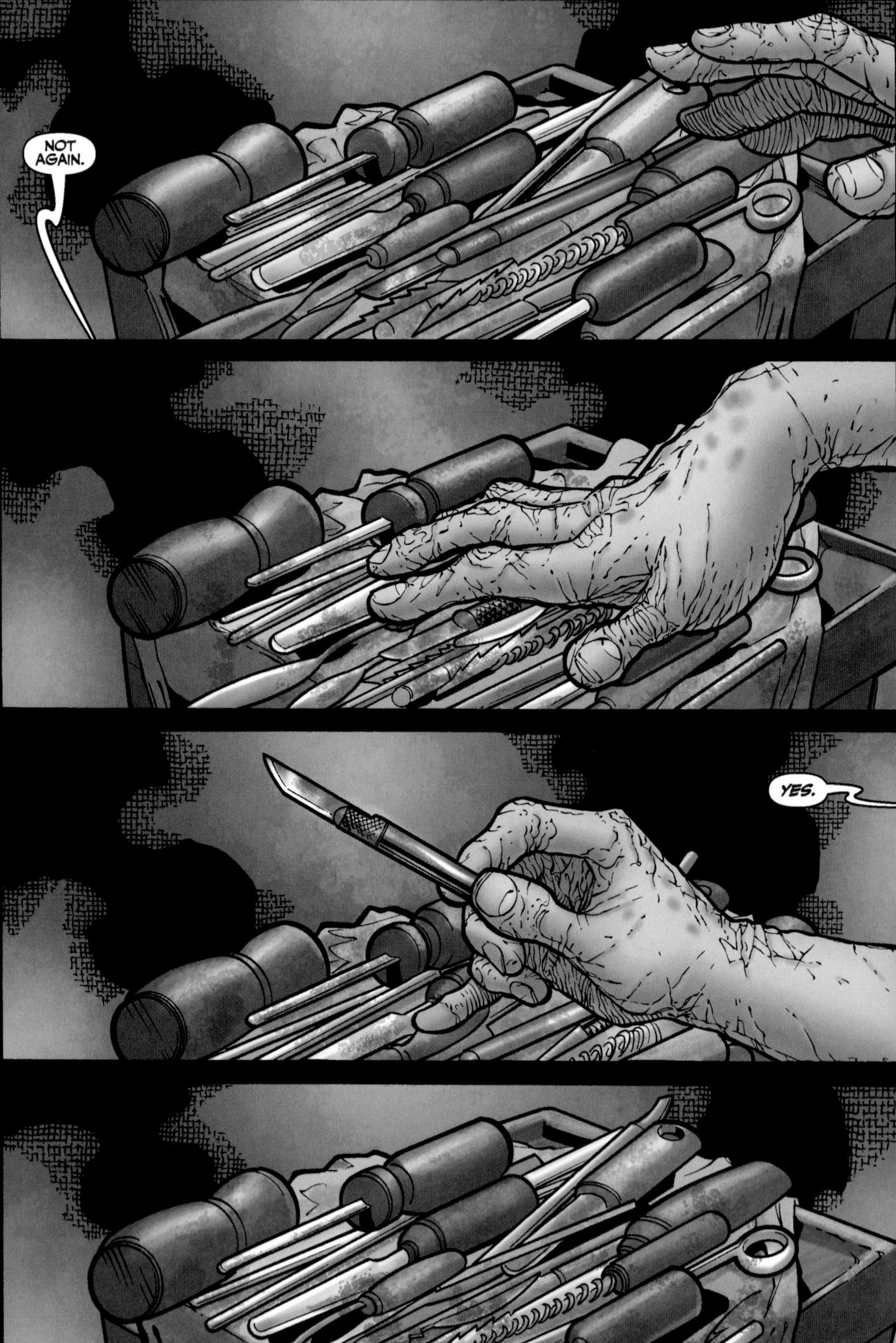
NOT AGAIN.
YES.

AGAIN.

HOW LONG ARE YOU GOING TO KEEP DOING THIS TO ME?
I TOLD YOU.
UNTIL YOU'RE SAFE.

I'M GENERALLY OKAY WITH MOST OF THE THINGS DAWN'S *NOT.*

SHE'S NOT PUNCTUAL, NOT TIDY, SHE'S VERY NOT GOOD ABOUT RETURNING THE ***VERONICA MARS*** D.V.D.'S I FINALLY GOT TO PLAY ON MY STUPID SCOTTISH PLAYER...
SO AWESOME. END OF SEASON TWO, THEY--
DON'T TELL ME.

BUT *"HERE,"* IS ON THE LIST NOW, AS IN *"DAWN IS NOT HERE."* AND THAT WORRIES ME.
WHAT'S THE BIG? SHE PROBABLY GALLOPED OFF WITH A FEW WOODLAND BUDDIES TO, I DUNNO, SOW SOME WILD OATS--METAPHORICALLY OR OTHERWISE. WE WERE YOUNG ONCE, REMEMBER?

HONESTLY, NO. AND THE BIG IS, IF LATEST INTEL IS EVEN REMOTELY ACCURATE, WE GOT A SPLINTER ARMY OF VAMPS LED BY JUDAS CRADLE ...
HATE HIM.

VAMP ARMY SWEEPING THE COUNTRYSIDE. AND OUR FRIEND FLICKA OUT THERE ALONE. WE HAVE TO RESCUE DAWN, AND I DON'T MEAN THE UNDERRATED CHRISTIAN BALE MOVIE.

I WANT TO GET MY SISTER TO SAFETY TOO. CAN'T. NOT NOW. THE THREAT OUTSIDE'S TOO BIG TO EVERY SLAYER I'VE GOT HERE. I MEAN, LOOK AT ME. WHO DRESSES LIKE WOLVERINE FOR FUN?
CERTAINLY NOT ME.

ANY PROOF YOU'VE SEEN TO THE CONTRARY COULD HAVE EASILY BEEN PHOTOSHOPPED, AND BESIDES, I WAS DRUNK.
IT'S MY FAULT. IF I'D SPENT A LITTLE TIME BEING MORE SISTER THAN SLAYER, MAYBE DAWN WOULDN'T NEED TO TROT OFF WITH HER FOREST BUDDIES FOR DAYS AT A TIME.

TIME OUT. YOU'RE BEING TOO HARSH ON YOURSELF. YOU'RE NOT A SLAYER, YOU'RE *THE* SLAYER, AND EVERY SOLDIER HERE NEEDS YOU. ALSO: TEENAGERS. LIKE TO RUN FREE. FOUR-LEGGED ONES PROBABLY TWICE AS MUCH.

IT'S NOT LIKE *YOU* PUT THE SPELL ON HER.
HELLO? COMMAND CENTRAL? WAR COMING, THE EYE PATCH IS STAYIN'.
WHEN THIS IS OVER, THINGS ARE GONNA BE DIFFERENT BETWEEN THE SUMMERS GIRLS. FIRST, THINK YOU CAN SPLINTER OFF, TAKE A RECON GROUP, FIND HER?
BESIDES, YOURS TRULY PLANNED AHEAD. I MAY NOT FIND DAWN, BUT I KNOW A GUY WHO CAN HELP.
YOU DO? I LOVE YOU. HOW?

I HAVE AN ACE IN MY HOLE. LET ME INSTANTLY REPHRASE THAT. WE HAVE...

"...AN INSIDE MAN."
DING DONG

HELLO. I'M A COLLEGE STUDENT ATTENDING COLLEGE...

...WHO COINCIDENTALLY ALSO NEEDS A ROOM-MATE, COMPLETELY BY COINCIDENCE, AND THEN I SAW YOUR AD. I'M IN.
SO, YO, WHAT'S THE RENT, BRO?

WHERE...

...DO YOU THINK YOU'RE GOING?
YOU KNOW WHAT'S BETTER THAN STAYING HERE? ESCAPING. COME ON.
WHY WOULD YOU WANT TO LEAVE?
HE MADE US. HE'S OUR FATHER. WE'RE HOME.
I HAD A SPELL PUT ON ME.
YOU'RE DIFFERENT.
YOU CAN'T LEAVE.
YOU CAN NEVER LEAVE.

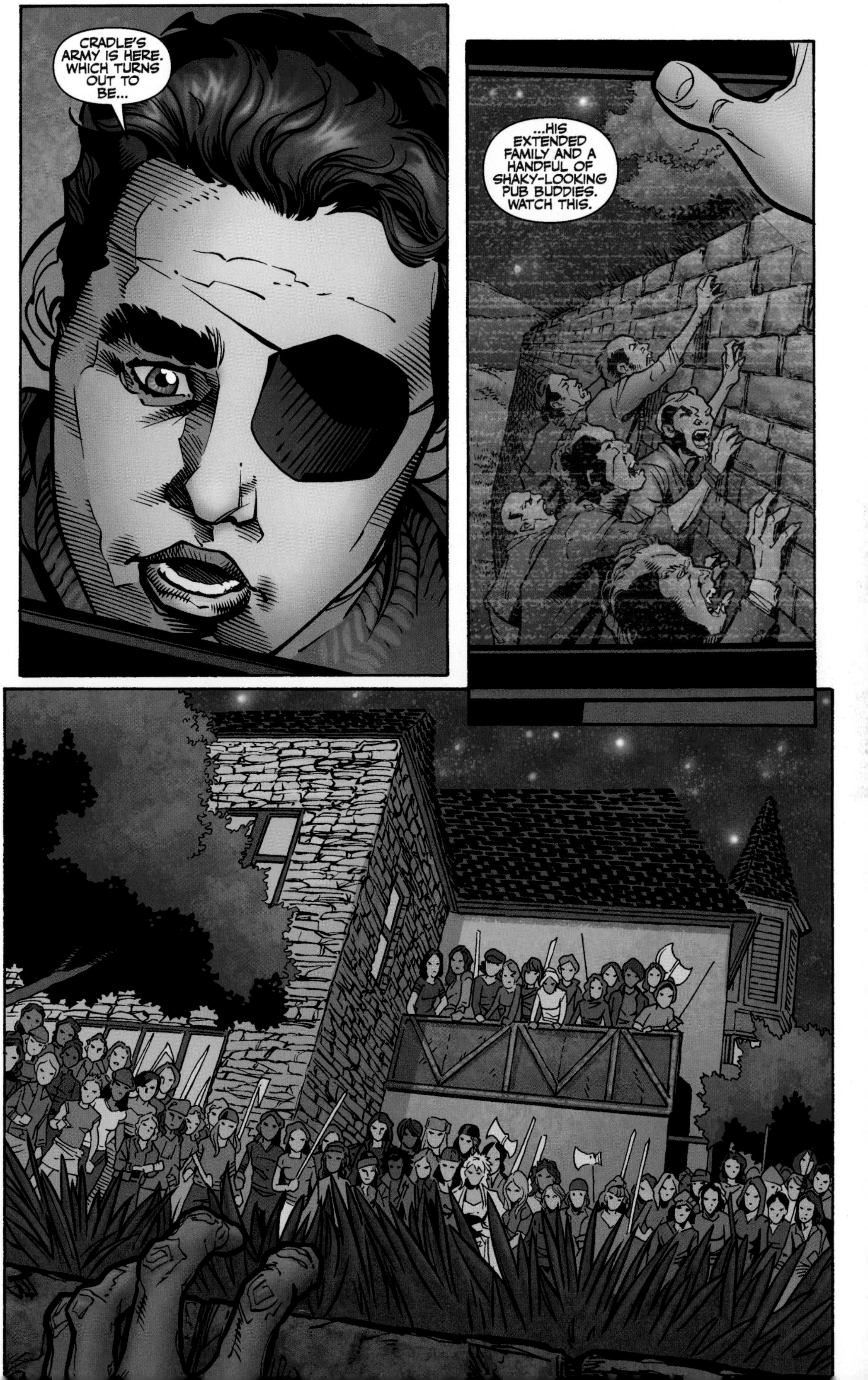

CRADLE'S ARMY IS HERE. WHICH TURNS OUT TO BE...

...HIS EXTENDED FAMILY AND A HANDFUL OF SHAKY-LOOKING PUB BUDDIES. WATCH THIS.

THAT WENT WELL.
LET'S FIND DAWN.
...MY POINT BEING, YOU HAD MORE PEOPLE TO TALK TO THAN DAWN DOES NOW WHEN YOU WERE HER AGE. YOUR MOM, GILES, ME, WILL...
I ALSO HAD A LOT OF PEOPLE WORRYING ABOUT ME, ALL THE TIME. I WANTED THINGS TO BE DIFFERENT FOR DAWN.
THEY ARE DIFFERENT. IT'S WEIRD, IT'S LIKE SHE'S A WHOLE DIFFERENT PERSON. BECAUSE, OH, SHE IS. AND AS FOR PEOPLE WORRYING ABOUT YOU: YOU WERE ALMOST KILLED, A LOT. TWICE FOR REALS. SO, THE WORRY: NOT UNJUSTIFIED.

HEY, YOU KNOW HOW YOU DON'T WANT DAWN TO THINK YOU'RE WORRYING?
WORRY.
TRACKS DISAPPEARED?
WORSE. TRANSMOGRIFIED. AND WE'RE INTO PHASE THREE.
AND NOW I'M ALARMED. GET THE THRICEWISE. HAVE WILLOW TRANSPORT HIM IMMEDIATELY.
THIS SPELL TOOK WORK. HOW DANGEROUS IS THIS KENNY?
HARD TO SAY. YOU DON'T USUALLY GET THIS STRONG A SPELL FROM THE THRICEWISE COMMUNITY. APPARENTLY, HE'S A NICE GUY WHO JUST SNAPPED AFTER DAWN BOINKED HIS ROOMMATE.
HOW CAN I NOT KNOW THIS?
IT CANNOT BE BECAUSE I JUST TOLD YOU BECAUSE I WOULD NEVER DO THAT. BUGGER.
HEY, CHECK ME OUT, NOW I CAN HATE MYSELF IN BRITISH.

DON'T BE ANGRY. IT'S NOT THEIR FAULT.

MAGICKS WITH A "K." THAT'S WHAT I'M TALKING ABOUT. I GOT EXPELLED FROM WESLEYAN FOR "DABBLING." WHEN YOUR FEMINIST-STUDIES PROFESSOR ACCUSES YOU OF WITCHCRAFT, YOU GOTTA BE ONTO SOMETHING. SO. KNOW ANYBODY ON CAMPUS WHO'S INTO TOASTING UP SOME TASTY BUDS OF SOR-CER-Y?

UM, I KNOW A LITTLE ABOUT MAGICKS, ACTUALLY. LIKE, THE FACT THAT YOU ARE PLACING TOTEMS AROUND THE ROOM RIGHT NOW. WHY?
TOTEMS? FOR WHAT, AND I MEAN, WHAT ARE THOSE ANYWAY?

WE'RE MADE.
THEY DON'T HAVE ANYTHING TO DO WITH SETTING A MYSTICAL TELEPORTATION GRID, I CAN TELL YOU THAT RIGHT NOW.
TOTEMS IN PLACE?
AYE.

EREHAVOTEG!

OH. HEAD RUSH.
CAN I JUST SAY ONE THING? "OH CRAP, HE GOT AWAY."
NO, WAIT.
YOU SAY THAT.

THING IN THE TREES STILL TRAILING US?
YUP.
TOK
NO. NO, NO, YOU DO NOT TALK TO ME ABOUT BREAKING THE TRUCE BETWEEN WOOD FOLK AND HUMANS WHEN YOU'VE BEEN TRAILING US FOR HALF AN HOUR. TEENY-TINY PEOPLE TRACKS. DISAPPEARED. WHERE'D THEY GO? WHO'D WANT A LITTLE GAL AROUND HERE?
WAS KINDA HOPING.
I'LL TELL YOU NOTHING!
KRRREERSHH
UH, THAT'S WEIRD. YOU JUST BROKE SOMEBODY'S WINDOW.

COTTAGE. OUT HERE. SHOW OF HANDS, WHO THINKS THAT'S CREEPY? BUT HERE'S MY REAL QUESTION:
WHAT ARE THESE TINY ARROWS DOING IN MY NECK?
YOU OKAY?
SURE. A LITTLE... POISONED, MAYBE...
AND OBVIOUSLY, BUFFY IS HERE.

LOOKS LIKE MY CHANCE TO BUST OUT OF THE VALLEY OF THE DOLLS...
NOW!
CRAP ON A STICK.
BUFFY!
I NEVER WANTED IT TO GO THIS FAR.
LET ME HELP.

BBWAAWK
PUT HER DOWN.
KEN?

DAWNIE.
KENNY, I'M SORRY.
POOF!

OKAY THIS IS AWKWARD, BUT HERE GOES: I'M SORRY I CAST A SPELL ON YOU THAT TURNED YOU INTO A GIANT, A CENTAUR, AND A CREEPY PORCELAIN DOLL.

IF I HADN'T SAID *"I'M SORRY,"* WHAT WOULD HAVE HAPPENED? WOULD I JUST KEEP TURNING INTO DIFFERENT BEINGS ENDLESSLY?

NOT ENDLESSLY. I WOULD HAVE CALLED IT OFF WHEN IT GOT TO THE HORNED FIRE SNAILS.

I'M SORRY I SLEPT WITH YOUR ROOMMATE.

WHY DOES THAT ONE SOUND SO MUCH MORE PAINFUL?
I THOUGHT YOU LIKED ME, LIKE THAT.
I WAS SCARED.
I HAD, HAVE, VERY INTENSE FEELINGS FOR YOU. SEX WOULD HAVE BEEN AT LEAST EQUALLY INTENSE, AND I WASN'T READY. NOT THEN.
I GET IT. I'M SORRY, TOO.

GOODBYE.

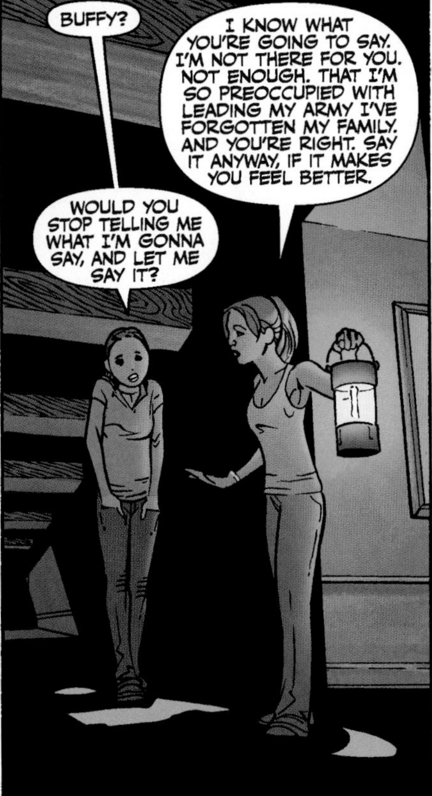
BUFFY?
I KNOW WHAT YOU'RE GOING TO SAY. I'M NOT THERE FOR YOU. NOT ENOUGH. THAT I'M SO PREOCCUPIED WITH LEADING MY ARMY I'VE FORGOTTEN MY FAMILY. AND YOU'RE RIGHT. SAY IT ANYWAY, IF IT MAKES YOU FEEL BETTER.
WOULD YOU STOP TELLING ME WHAT I'M GONNA SAY, AND LET ME SAY IT?

YOU CAN'T KEEP ME SAFE.
AND YOU DON'T HAVE TO.

WELL THAT'S JUST--WHAT'S THE WORD? STUPID. I'M YOUR SISTER.
YOU'RE THE SLAYER.
LOT OF THOSE, THESE DAYS.
NO. JUST ONE.
I KNEW KENNY WAS A THRICEWISE. DATED HIM ANYWAY. PISSED HIM OFF. PAUSE FOR REQUISITE TOLD YOU SO...
TOLD YOU SO.
...AND DID IT ANYWAY. MAYBE I WANTED YOU TO SAVE ME. A FEW YEARS AGO, YOU WERE THE ONLY SLAYER, I WAS YOUR ONLY SISTER. NOW I'M SURROUNDED BY, LIKE, A THOUSAND SORTA-LITTLE-SISTERS I CAN'T POSSIBLY COMPETE WITH. THEY FIGHT IN YOUR ARMY, THEY ALL COME EQUIPPED WITH FANCY NEW SUPERPOWERS AND WOULD LITERALLY DIE TO GET YOUR ATTENTION.
IT SUCKS.
SOUNDS LIKE. BUT TURNING YOURSELF INTO A GIANT, A HORSEY, AND A RAG DOLL IS BEYOND YOUR NORMAL PASSIVE-AGGRESSIVE.
COULD HAVE BEEN WORSE. FIRE SNAILS. JUST SAYIN'.
YOU'RE RIGHT. ABOUT ALL OF IT. BUT--AND I LOVE SAYING THIS--YOU'RE WRONG ABOUT ONE THING.
I GOT A THOUSAND SOLDIERS. ONLY ONE SISTER. I CAN'T KEEP HER SAFE AND IT MAKES ME CRAZY. BUT I LOVE HER.
I LOVE MY SISTER TO DEATH.
WON'T COME TO THAT.
NOT TONIGHT.
WANNA WATCH TV?
ONLY DESPERATELY.
I MIGHT HAVE SCRATCHED YOUR VERONICA MARS DISC...
AND I WILL KILL YOU.

The End

COVERS FROM

BUFFY THE VAMPIRE SLAYER

ISSUES #22–#25

By

GEORGES JEANTY

with

DEXTER VINES & MICHELLE MADSEN

·GEORGES·

BUFFY THE VAMPIRE SLAYER

SHORT STORIES FROM

MYSPACE DARK HORSE PRESENTS

"Harmony Bites"

Script JANE ESPENSON

Pencils KARL MOLINE

Inks ANDY OWENS

"Vampy Cat Play Friend"

Script STEVEN S. DEKNIGHT

Art CAMILLA D'ERRICO

Colors MICHELLE MADSEN

Letters RICHARD STARKINGS
& COMICRAFT'S JIMMY BETANCOURT

SCRIPT JANE ESPENSON
PENCILS KARL MOLINE
INKS ANDY OWENS COLORS MICHELLE MADSEN
LETTERS RICHARD STARKINGS & COMICRAFT'S JIMMY BETANCOURT

BUFFY THE VAMPIRE SLAYER™ © 2009 TWENTIETH CENTURY FOX FILM CORPORATION. ALL RIGHTS RESERVED.

"I HAVE A JOB INTERVIEW TONIGHT. THEY'RE LOOKING FOR A NEW BARTENDER AT THE HOUSE OF BLUES."
HOUSE OF BLUES
WELCOME TO THE HOUSE

I HOPE THEY DON'T EXPECT ME TO KNOW HOW TO *MIX DRINKS.*

I THINK PEOPLE WILL LIKE THAT I DON'T KNOW WHAT I'M DOING. IT'S FOLKSY AND IDENTIFIABLE.

"I THOUGHT THAT WAS GOING TO BE THE WORST PART OF THE NIGHT. BUT I DIDN'T KNOW WHAT WAS ABOUT TO HAPPEN."

JUSTIN!

I SIRED JUSTIN, LIKE, FOUR MONTHS AGO. YOU THINK HE'D BE GRATEFUL. BUT IT TURNS OUT HE WAS REALLY INTO TANNING.

"VAMPIRES CAN *STAKE* OTHER VAMPIRES, YOU KNOW, AND I DIDN'T LIKE THE WAY HE WAS FEELING UP THE FENCE.

KRAK

"SOMETIMES A STAKE IS POINTY AT *BOTH* ENDS."

KRSSSHHH

CLEM! YOU HAVE TO COME PICK ME UP!

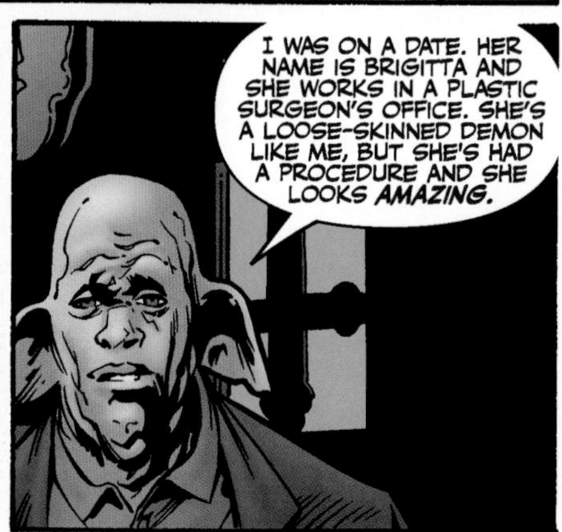
I WAS ON A DATE. HER NAME IS BRIGITTA AND SHE WORKS IN A PLASTIC SURGEON'S OFFICE. SHE'S A LOOSE-SKINNED DEMON LIKE ME, BUT SHE'S HAD A PROCEDURE AND SHE LOOKS AMAZING.

IT WAS SO UPSETTING. HE SHOULD'VE BEEN GRATEFUL, YOU KNOW? I HEAR THAT IN THE OLD-TIMEY TIMES IF YOU SIRED SOMEONE, THEY HAD TO BE YOUR BUTLER FOR A YEAR. IT WAS JUST COMMON CURTSY.
"WE DROPPED OFF THE TIGHT GIRL AND CLEM TOOK ME OUT FOR PINKBERRY IN WEST HOLLYWOOD. THEN HE THREW ME UNDER A BUS. A BUS MADE OF WORDS."

WHAT?!
I'M JUST SAYING, HE MIGHT HAVE HAD A POINT. SOMETIMES YOU USE PEOPLE.
"I THOUGHT CLEM WAS MY FRIEND."

Who's right in the fight? Text us your answer!

01) Harm's right–Clem needs to stay out of her business.

02) Clem's right–The she-vamp needs a revamp.

I'M SO MAD AT HIM I COULD KILL HIM.

IT WOULDN'T BE HARD.

METRO
917
963
33
SHE'S JUST HIGH STRUNG. SHE'S UNDER A LOT OF PRESSURE, BEING PRETTY AND FAMOUS. I KNOW SHE'D NEVER REALLY HURT ME.

I CAN BITE HIM. I CAN DRAIN HIM.

YEAH, I AM A BIT COLD AND STICKY. BUT I HAVE MY KNITTING BAG, AND THERE'S A SWEATER HERE THAT I'VE ALMOST FINISHED...

I'LL JUMP HIM WHEN HE GETS HOME.

I CAN HEAR HIM JUST OUTSIDE. THAT'S HIS KEY IN THE LOCK...

HARM? OH! OW! GAHH!

MY SWEATER!

WE HAD TO LAUGH.
AND THEN WE WERE FRIENDS AGAIN.
WE HAVE A CRAZY LIFE LIKE THAT.

HELLO?

I GOT THE BARTENDING JOB AT *THE HOUSE OF BLUES!*

"Next week, on Harmony Bites:"

THIS JOB IS REALLY HARD. I'M FREAKING OUT.

THE MANAGEMENT WANTS ME IN VAMP FACE ALL THE TIME AS A KIND OF NOVELTY, BUT IT'S HARD TO STAY THAT MAD, SO I'VE INVITED A BUNCH OF SLAYERS TO COME FOR MY FIRST NIGHT.

DO YOU THINK THAT'S A BAD IDEA?
The End

Buffy the Vampire Slayer™ © 2009 Twentieth Century Fox Film Corp. All rights reserved.

GRRRRR!

AIIIEEEEE!
MOTHER! MAKE IT STOP!
AHHOOO! IT HURTS!

SACHIKO IS AGAIN HAPPY!
GRRR!
OW!
I COULD NOT HELP IT! YOU'RE JUST SO SWEET!
I LOVE YOU, VAMPY CAT!
HAPPY ENDING BROUGHT TO YOU BY YOUR FRIENDS AT THE SANTORIO CORPORATION!

ADVERTISEMENT

HARM

SLAYERS:
Why they
HATE
America

HARM'S CLOSET:
BEYOND GOTH TO GLAM

EXCLUSIVE
Q&A
with REALITY STAR
HARMONY KENDALL

Buffy the Vampire Slayer

HARMONY BITES
SEASON PREMIERE
Wednesday, January 7
Check with local retailers for showtimes.
Bonus episode on myspace.com/darkhorsepresents!

Buffy the Vampire Slayer™ © 2008, 2009 Twentieth Century Fox Film Corporation. All rights reserved.

Q&A

with Harmony Kendall

We sat down with sultry vampire Harmony Kendall, the up-and-coming reality-TV star, whose hot new show follows this vixen vampire on her many exploits—bloodsucking, pampering her Pomeranians, and partying it up in LA's trendiest clubs.

How did you come up with the concept for the reality show *Harmony Bites*?
It wasn't very hard. I looked at all the other reality shows and made mine just like theirs, pretty much. Which is how they made theirs, I'm sure. So I guess it all goes back to that big original reality show we call reality. Or "Survivor."

Was it a tough choice between *Harmony Bites* and *Harmony Sucks*?
No. Duh. *Harmony Bites* rules! *Harmony Sucks* bites!

Does the sudden popularity surprise you, or did you always know vampires would have their day in the, er . . . sun?
I don't respond to dot-dot-dot puns. They're disingenuous. That being said, it is about time that the evil side of the scale got some love. If you need both, you need both, you know?

How do your friends and family feel about your newly gained fame?
My friends and family were cast for me by the production company to fill out the show, so they're all very psyched about it.

"I'VE BEEN TOYING WITH THE IDEA OF MAKING A PACT WITH THE FORCES BELOW . . ."

With all of the bloodsucking that you have to accomplish to keep viewers engaged, how do you maintain your physique? Blood: fattening?
I don't recommend a blood diet for the "look at me, I breathe air" crowd, but for the undead, it's the way to go. Add yoga for an almost-alive glow.

What's the best part about being a vampire?
Oh, gosh, it's all pretty sweet. Everyone talks about the eternal youth, but I think that ignores the importance of superhuman strength. Think about it. The stronger you are, the more you can lift. So being strong is like living in a world where everything's light. It's sweet!

What's next for Harmony Kendall?
I've been toying with the idea of making a pact with the forces below and tapping into some very dark energy at the world-destroying level. There's also a possibility of a country-music album, but all spoken-word, like a sort of country-rap thing.

VISIT ME at myspace.com/harmonybites

HARMONY BITES SEASON PREMIERE, Wednesday, January 7

Buffy the Vampire Slayer™ © 2008, 2009 Twentieth Century Fox Film Corporation. All rights reserved

SLAYERS: WHY THEY HATE AMERICA

They have bases around the world, they look just like us, and they're on a mission. Their goal is nothing less than deciding for the rest of us what kind of people meet their limited definition of "human" and persecuting anyone who doesn't make the list. This is the Slayer Army, and they're just as scary as their name, determined to destroy our cherished way of life.

Don't believe us? Take a trip to Southern California. An hour east of LA, there's a giant crater where the idyllic town of Sunnydale used to sit. Once it was a beautiful suburban paradise, a slice of authentic small-town America. Real America. With a malt shop. But then the Slayers came, from all over the world, even the weird countries, and now there's nothing left.

Let's not risk another Sunnydale. Look closely at your sisters, your girlfriend or wife, your mother. Any of them could be a Slayer . . . Stay alert, and (continued on page 20)

VAMPY CAT! GRRR! ARGH! HE'LL LOVE YOU TO DEATH!

On sale **FEBRUARY 4** from your friends at the SANTORIO CORPORATION!

HARMONY BITES SEASON PREMIERE

WEDNESDAY, JANUARY 7
Check with local retailers for showtimes

Bonus Episode on myspace.com/darkhorsepresents!

BUFFY #21 AVAILABLE AT YOUR LOCAL COMICS SHOP
To find a comics shop in your area, call 1-888-266-4226 | For more information or to order direct, visit darkhorse.com or call 1-800-862-0052

Buffy the Vampire Slayer™ © 2008, 2009 Twentieth Century Fox Film Corporation. All rights reserved.

TOP THREE SLAYER PUBLIC ENEMIES

#1: BUFFY

She brought the reign of Slayers down upon the creatures of the night, and will stop at nothing to bring down the vampires and demons of the world—even vampires who only drink the blood of the living as a recreational habit, not to kill! She is cunning, unforgiving, and completely out of touch when it comes to what the world now wants and needs. Once a trend-setter, this Slayer has fallen behind the times.

#2: FAITH

At one time a friend to creatures of the night, this rogue Slayer seems to have obtained some "clarity"—she's out to discover Slayers who have lost their way (meaning they don't want to *be* "chosen" and prefer to live a quiet, normal life like the rest of us). Faith can't leave well enough alone, and while she doesn't follow Buffy's military-style regiment, she's helping young, innocent girls become warriors, killers, and monsters in their own right.

#3: KENNEDY

Hotheaded and overly confident, this "next-gen" Slayer is a fierce fighter and one of Buffy's closest allies. She's often abrasive and focused on the prize—the killing of innocent, yet bloodthirsty, vampires.

FROM JOSS WHEDON

BUFFY THE VAMPIRE SLAYER SEASON 8:

VOLUME 1: THE LONG WAY HOME
Joss Whedon and Georges Jeanty
ISBN 978-1-59307-822-5 | $15.95

VOLUME 2: NO FUTURE FOR YOU
Brian K. Vaughan, Georges Jeanty, and Joss Whedon
ISBN 978-1-59307-963-5 | $15.95

VOLUME 3: WOLVES AT THE GATE
Drew Goddard, Georges Jeanty, and Joss Whedon
ISBN 978-1-59582-165-2 | $15.95

VOLUME 4: TIME OF YOUR LIFE
Joss Whedon, Jeph Loeb, Georges Jeanty, and others
ISBN 978-1-59582-310-6 | $15.95

VOLUME 5: PREDATORS AND PREY
Joss Whedon, Jane Espenson, Cliff Richards, Georges Jeanty, and others
ISBN 978-1-59582-342-7 | $15.95

TALES OF THE SLAYERS
Joss Whedon, Amber Benson, Gene Colan, P. Craig Russell, Tim Sale, and others
ISBN 978-1-56971-605-2 | $14.95

TALES OF THE VAMPIRES
Joss Whedon, Brett Matthews, Cameron Stewart, and others
ISBN 978-1-56971-749-3 | $15.95

FRAY: FUTURE SLAYER
Joss Whedon and Karl Moline
ISBN 978-1-56971-751-6 | $19.95

SERENITY VOLUME 1: THOSE LEFT BEHIND
Joss Whedon, Brett Matthews, and Will Conrad
ISBN 978-1-59307-449-4 | $9.95

SERENITY VOLUME 2: BETTER DAYS
ISBN 978-1-59582-162-1 | $9.95

ALSO FROM DARK HORSE . . .

BUFFY THE VAMPIRE SLAYER OMNIBUS

VOLUME 1
ISBN 978-1-59307-784-6 | $24.95

VOLUME 2
ISBN 978-1-59307-826-3 | $24.95

VOLUME 3
ISBN 978-1-59307-885-0 | $24.95

VOLUME 4
ISBN 978-1-59307-968-0 | $24.95

VOLUME 5
ISBN 978-1-59582-225-3 | $24.95

VOLUME 6
ISBN 978-1-59582-242-0 | $24.95

VOLUME 7
ISBN 978-1-59582-331-1 | $24.95

BUFFY THE VAMPIRE SLAYER: PANEL TO PANEL
ISBN 978-1-59307-836-2 | $19.95

MYSPACE DARK HORSE PRESENTS, VOLUME 1
Featuring "Sugarshock" by Joss Whedon and Fábio Moon
ISBN 978-1-59307-998-7 | $17.95

DARK HORSE BOOKS®
darkhorse.com

Buffy the Vampire Slayer™ & © 1998, 2009 Twentieth Century Fox Film Corporation. All rights reserved. Fray™ & © 2009 Joss Whedon. Serenity: Those Left Behind © 2009 Universal Studios Licensing LLLP. The movie "Serenity" © Universal Studios. All rights reserved. (BL 5051)

AVAILABLE AT YOUR LOCAL COMICS SHOP OR BOOKSTORE!
To find a comics shop in your area, call 1-888-266-4226.
For more information or to order direct: • On the web: darkhorse.com • E-mail: mailorder@darkhorse.com • Phone: 1-800-862-0052
Mon.–Fri. 9 AM to 5 PM Pacific Time.
*Prices and availability subject to change without notice